MW01629582

WHEN NIGHTLIFE FALLS

Spacuna Publishing
P.O. Box 2029
Peekskill, NY 10566

Spacuna Publishing paperback edition, August 2011

Cover photo: Jeff Eason
Cover models: Erik Rhodes and Christopher Schram
Cover Design: Cynthia Mulligan

Hartley, Derek
As Nightlife Falls/Derek Hartley
ISBN 978-0-578-08945-4

Printed in the United States of America

"We're not just friends, we're Friendsters!"

In Memoriam:
Friendster.com
(2002 – 2011)

Contents

Introduction

I am pretty sure I had a nervous breakdown in 2007. Of course, if you aren't rolling around on the floor and frothing at the mouth, it might be kind of hard to tell. It wasn't a dragged off screaming into the snake pit kind of emotional collapse. It happened in slow motion like those time-lapsed photography films we had to watch in elementary school science class to show how plants grow or things decompose. It reminded me of one of my favorite lines from *Will & Grace* when Will asks Grace "Are you having your stroke in installments." I think I had a nervous breakdown in installments. Whatever it was, it was definitely pay as you go.

And there wasn't really anyone to talk to about it. My boyfriend of three years and I had broken up. My family was 3,000 miles away. My best friend Mike is not what I would call the warm-fuzzy-let's-talk-out-our-feelings type. My therapy is blathering on about nothing on my national radio show, which is usually enough to keep me, if not stable, then at least driving around in that neighborhood. But inside, I was a chaotic mess, even more than usual. My way of dealing with my midlife crisis, for lack of a better expression, was to do nothing until I reached my breaking point.

And then I impulse bought a house.

I used to own a small farmhouse in Michigan that I bought to be near my grandmother after she retired. At the time, I had just finished a few very profitable years at the height of the dot com boom at America Online and could afford to move away to the middle of nowhere and drop out of life for a while. But when I started working on the radio, I sold it since I knew it would be impossible to spend much time there once I was chained to a microphone five days a week. Since then, Mike and I had been living in a very nice two bedroom apartment in Harlem that was the envy of our friends. The inexpensive duplex had plenty of room, including a full dining room, and even a washer and dryer inside the apartment. If it had a second bathroom, a dishwasher in the kitchen and a mild reduction in city noise, we would still be there.

But I have always been terrible with money. So when I left AOL, I wisely poured most of what I had into that farmhouse by paying cash for the whole thing. In the end, it turned out to be a shrewd move because I didn't end up blowing through all of what I had on clothes that didn't fit very well or the latest piece of technology that would be forgotten or ignored a few months later. After I sold that first house, the money was just sitting in an interest-bearing account, which I would tap occasionally to pay for utter nonsense. As I watched it very slowly dwindle away on vacations and disposable crap, I realized that if I didn't pour it back into something solid, it would all be gone before I knew it.

My investing instincts in the stock market are notoriously bad so my best bet was pouring it all back into a house, which in the spring of 2007, I did. The housing market had already started to turn soft so I figured I could get a deal. Naturally, my instincts for real estate are about on par with my instincts for the stock market and a year later the entire real estate market collapsed as part of a row of falling dominoes that made up the worst financial disaster since the Great Depression. Timing is everything.

The end of the world was more than just a year away; it was a million miles from my thinking. I was much more concerned with losing my mind. So I focused my energy on choosing a new place to live. At first I wasn't sure of what kind of place to buy. When you live in New York City, you really only have three options. You can buy an apartment which will be a sixth of the size of what you could get for the same money in a house out of town. Your second option is a full time house a commutable distance from the city. Or you can split the difference, keep your rental in the city and buy a weekend house more than an hour away that you only see during the summer.

I immediately ruled out buying an apartment in the city. When I first got to Manhattan in January 2001, my friend Tony talked me out of buying a compact one bedroom on the eastside of midtown for $190,000. By the time I started looking again six years later, that same apartment would run closer to $500,000 if I could even find it. It seemed ridiculous to pay that kind of money when I could get something huge outside the city for the same money and not feel like I was living in a gerbil's habit trail. I liked the idea of a summer place as well as the theme song to *A Summer Place* but I traveled all summer long for work so that didn't make any practical sense at all.

So I settled about trying to find a place outside the city that was a reasonable, commutable distance from Manhattan. Immediately, I ruled out New Jersey and Long Island. The commuter train situation into the city didn't thrill me. So it was Connecticut or upstate New York. Connecticut seemed too far and what was available closer in the state was just too expensive. So I turned to Westchester County, the cozy suburban enclave north of the city that is home to Martha Stewart and the Clintons. I wanted an older house with character in an established neighborhood, plenty of bedrooms and bathrooms, preferably walking distance to the train to the city, and what had been lacking so much in the city: quiet. Basically, I was doing that thing that you always do when you get out of a relationship: run to the exact opposite of what you just had, trying in vain to fix the mistakes from the past. It doesn't work, by the way.

After a couple of trips around looking at various places, I found a cute Cape Cod online and my realtor and I went to look at it. It was on the corner of a quarter acre lot in a quiet suburban neighborhood. It had a fully built out basement which Mike wanted to stake out as his own. I would be on the second floor. With our conflicting schedules, we would basically never see each other again. It had the things I wanted and I even went so far as to measure the place for possible furniture placement, but I thought the price might be a little high so I wanted to see a comparison house to make sure it was a good deal.

When I checked again, there was suddenly another 1950s Cape Cod online that was in the same town, the same number of bedrooms (four) and bathrooms (two) on a third of an acre for the same price. So I asked my realtor to take me to see it just to see how it compared. Well, there was no comparison. As we drove up the hill, I marveled at how nice the other houses on the street were. “Oh my God,” I thought to myself, “Rich people live here.”

The house itself was adorable, tiny from the street, but as we walked through it turned out to be deceptively roomy. Where the other house had counted its walk-out basement in the square footage, this house did not, making it almost a third larger. As soon as we stepped down into the basement and saw the classic rec room bar, I knew this was the house. It was a done deal. The owners had just lowered the price that Tuesday and I saw it on a Thursday. I knew if I didn’t make an offer on Friday, someone else would during the planned open house on Saturday. I was in.

But little did I know that I would be sacrificing my life for the sake of saving my sanity.

The Grouchy Oscar

Monday, February 26th - I like to throw parties, although I tend to throw them with the kind of intensity usually reserved for curve balls at the World Series or Soviet era directives from the Kremlin. It's mandatory fun for all! Anyone who has been to one of my parties can attest to the great selection of food, fun people and, more importantly, top shelf liquor. But perhaps in a more hushed tone they will describe my Crawford-esque mania for proper behavior. I am incapable of hiding my emotions, especially my darkest ones. And when people get out of line at a party, my sudden appearance on the scene might remind one of a surprise inspection by a prison warden.

In the years since I moved to New York City, I have been well known for two parties: Cinco de Mayo and the Oscars. Even though I am often found scrambling for something to do on that night, I am wary of throwing New Year's Eve parties because there is so much strategy involved in being at the "right" party at midnight. If people don't like the crowd where they are, they will abandon you like rats off a ship just before eleven, and you might be left with a case of unopened champagne and an empty apartment as the New Year begins. Not the way people generally like to kick things off.

My first (and last) New Year's Eve party at the apartment included my roommate breaking up with his boyfriend on the front steps (not exactly welcoming) and me left with six open but barely touched bottles of champagne. The latter made me the most crazy. I am convinced that champagne, like sex in a car, is the kind of thing that sounds like a lot more fun in the abstract than it actually is. People love the idea of champagne, but as liquor experiences go, it belongs in a bygone era with opera and horse-drawn carriages.

It is one thing to have some champagne left over in a single bottle after your party is over. You just pour it out. It is wasteful but you can't put a cork in it like wine or save it for your next party like vodka. Having people look at five open bottles of champagne, not like the selection and then open a sixth for a parting sip on their way to a better party is purely rotten. They might as well have crowned me with the bottle on their way out. Suffice it to say, as I poured hundreds of dollars worth of champagne down the sink at 12:15am in an empty apartment, I vowed never to have another New Year's Eve party.

I started throwing Cinco de Mayo parties when I was living out in LA before the big move east. In Manhattan, Cinco de Mayo is as remote as the moon, so there is very little competition. And if the gays love one thing almost as much as the love/hate relationship they have with themselves, they love any excuse to drink a margarita. There is nothing to throwing a Cinco de Mayo party. Some pitchers of margaritas, a few cases of Corona and a hearty stack of tortilla chips and your theme is complete. Naturally, I take it a few notches up from there but any college student returning from spring break in Cancun with a few tacky souvenirs can throw a party a month later that will be the envy of their friends with minimal investment and not much imagination.

I had initially hoped to close on my house so fast that we wouldn't still be in our apartment in the city anymore when it came time for the Oscars, let alone Cinco de Mayo. But despite how ready I was and how distressed the seller originally seemed, suddenly things were moving very slowly. The husband was having health problems and disentangling themselves from seventeen years in a four-bedroom house to a much smaller condo somewhere else was apparently a daunting task. Very quickly, it seemed like the soonest we would be closing would be April, perhaps May. So I went ahead and planned my Oscar party as usual and figured it would be the Cinco de Mayo party I would have to skip.

I really like throwing Oscar parties. Well, I should say that I liked throwing them. When it came to theme, I knew that I could outdo anyone I knew. From my years working at Sony Pictures, I had snagged an official Oscar poster, the final design from the late great Saul Bass (most famous for doing credit sequences and mapping out the *Psycho* shower scene for Hitchcock). I also had movie posters for our big Oscar movies that year: our documentary on Anne Frank that won and *Sense and Sensibility* which lost out to *Braveheart* for Best Picture.

In addition to my well-placed Oscar posters, my friend Tony on a trip to Europe brought back a pair of golden salt and pepper shakers in the shape of Oscar. I cherish them even though they are a flagrant violation of the Academy's copyright. Legal issues aside, they always had a prominent place in the center of my dining room table on Oscar night.

I always say that no one cares about the food at your party as long as there is plenty of liquor. While this is true, I do like to put some thought into the spread. After all, if people just drink and don't eat, trouble happens. With the Oscars, I like to put together a full selection of movie theater food. The dining room table, slammed up against the wall buffet-style is overburdened with a make your own nachos and hot dog bar. Drunken people love the bubbling crock pot of glowing orange cheese sauce. Trust me. It is a nice touch, even if its nutritional value is beyond suspect.

On the sideboard, I put fresh popped popcorn and cases of candy bars and licorice. Naturally, there is also a wide selection of sodas but the real winner is the liquor. Always top shelf and always in abundance, there is nothing more important. I like to have at least six different kinds of beer on hand, in addition to all the primary and secondary liquors. When people ask what I have to drink and I say "everything" as a reply, I want to mean it.

I tend to vigorously dissuade people from bringing anything to one of my parties. This is for good reason. I plan these parties out very precisely, in particular when it comes to storage space. When you live in an apartment in Manhattan, space is always at a premium. There isn't additional room for your Zima no one wants to drink or strange appetizer that no one finds appetizing. The last party I threw in LA, someone brought a six pack of beer in cans and my sister, a stranger to gay parties, asked me why all the gay men kept reacting in horror when they opened the fridge. Last Thanksgiving, I walked into the kitchen to find the oven door open and my turkey exposed to the elements as my friend Chuck, during his brief unsuccessful flirtation with vegetarianism, trying to rearrange things to make room for his tofurkey. I could have strangled him with an oven mitt.

It was at that same Thanksgiving that I walked into the dining room to find paparazzi photographer James Edstrom clutching the corner of my antique card table that I had put up as a second table. "Look how wobbly it is," he cried out as he shook the edges of the table violently, nearly ripping the top off the base. I wanted to punch him in the throat so hard he would fall backwards out the dining room window. I won't be inviting him back.

I suppose on a certain level, this kind of outrageous behavior is my fault. I am a heavy pour and when gay men get drunk all bets are off. For a time, I thought Jell-O shots were fun to have at a party. And then, one year, my friend Randy got out of control and threw one of them at the wall between the kitchen and the living room. It didn't matter how many times we scrubbed that wall, the Jell-O never came out of the white paint. My friend Darin, aka Big and Silly, would get drunk, hide his lanky 6'8" frame under a tent of couch cushions on the sofa and then drag unsuspecting young men inside as they tried to walk by, like a spider enveloping its prey.

So I suppose I shouldn't have been surprised that the guests at the last Oscar party in my apartment all served to annoy me. First of all, one of my beloved Oscar salt and pepper shakers went missing. I don't know if someone broke it and didn't want to tell me or if they just snagged it as a souvenir but one of them was gone. I was heartbroken. They were literally irreplaceable and they had been a gift from one of my most treasured friends. Anyone will tell you that I am the definition of a sore winner when it comes to gifts. I hate getting them and if I hate the gift, I am not at all shy about making my displeasure known. Nothing discourages someone from ever getting you a gift again like opening the box and declared, "What made you get me something like this?" But I loved those shakers and to lose one of them was truly devastating.

But before I discovered that one of the shakers was missing, I had to endure the Oscar telecast. To help make both the Oscars and our lives in general better, I had purchased a wonderful 50 inch LCD rear projection TV. This was the envy of our friends since it was practically the size of some of their apartments and it cemented my Oscar party as the place to be. Unfortunately the addition of technology only ended up making it worse and not better.

With the TV we also had our beloved TiVo. I thought it would be great to be a bit behind during the show so that we could fast forward through the commercials but one of the guests vehemently objected. "No! We have to watch the commercials. That's why people watch the Oscars: for the commercials." No. That is why people watch the Super Bowl. People watch the Oscars for the stars, the gowns and the horrible mistakes and surprise upsets. With civil war breaking out in the living room, there was nothing to do but suffer through endless L'Oreal commercials (because we are worth it) to keep the peace.

But the worst thing about the Oscars was not actually being able to watch the show. If I wasn't in the kitchen checking on the food or making someone a drink, I was cleaning up a mess or getting trapped in conversation with someone who really just came for the liquor and the chance to meet a new guy. A sudden burst of laughter would erupt from the living room and I would round the corner in anticipation. "What happened?" I would ask, to a collective, "you missed it." No one volunteered to rewind anything so I could see it for myself, not even at my own party. That's it, I thought to myself as I dumped a fresh batch of steaming hot dogs onto a plate to deliver to the buffet in the living room. This is my last Oscar party. And it was.

I know it doesn't seem from all the complaining and horror stories but I really do love throwing parties. I like having people around. And I like the part where people come and have their own good time and at the end of the evening they tell me how much fun they had. I don't even need to see it happening. I just like knowing that it did happen. But I love the Oscars. Movies and TV are two of my favorite things and when they come together it is like *Hart to Hart*. Unfortunately, I can't seem to manage to enjoy the Oscars and throw a party at the same time. So something had to give. Cinco de Mayo will live on, but going forward, it will be me alone in front of the massive TV, fast-forwarding through boring speeches and rewinding to see my favorite moments again, because I am worth it.

Inspector Had It

Wednesday, March 28th - Buying a house is a little bit like falling in love. You are so excited in the first mad flushes of excitement that sometimes you don't see exactly what you are getting yourself into. But more than just falling in love, it is like falling in love on a reality show like *The Bachelor* because once you declare your feelings; you don't get to start your new life immediately. You have to wait weeks, or even months, to consummate everything. In the meantime, it is entirely possible that you could fall out of love just as easily as you fell in. I wasn't falling out of love by any stretch, but in my case, making a spontaneous purchase of a house meant I hadn't really thought through the details of what was happening or how my life would change. I loved our old apartment in Harlem but more than that, I was anxious to begin my new life out of the city, even if I wasn't exactly sure yet what that meant.

I saw the house on a Thursday and by Friday afternoon, I was submitting an offer. Perhaps I was overwhelmed by how much better that second house had been. Mostly, I think it was my own inherent cheapness. It felt like I was getting a sweet deal. So much house, far more than I rationally needed, for such a reasonable price. What can

I say? I can't resist a bargain and this seemed like one of the best I would find.

During the initial look at the house with my realtor, I was bowled over my how much bigger it was than either our apartment in the city or the other house I had considered. Yes, the upstairs bathroom looked like the scene of some kind of horrific crime, but didn't I say I wanted a bit of a fixer-upper I could make my own? And once I walked into the basement, all the tacky furnishings and pine paneling evaporated from my mind. There, sitting in a dark neglected corner was a bar.

Magically in my mind, the basement was transformed into the cool hangout of my dreams. It was just like the scene in Xanadu where the nightclub magically comes to life but without the weird musical number. I imagined the fabulous parties I would throw, the handsome gay men laughing and drinking as I shook up another batch of happiness in a cocktail shaker from which gallons of love would pour. Randy could throw all the Jell-O shots he wanted and who would care? In that moment of complete and utter delusion, I was sold.

I like to believe I kept my poker face intact. After all, you don't want to seem too excited in front of the other realtor and the seller. It makes it much harder to negotiate. My own realtor however couldn't keep it in his pants.

“Oh my God!” he had cried out, pulling me from my bar-induced reverie. “Look at these steel beams. If you don’t buy this house, I will!”

I could have whacked him in the head with those steel beams. Who does that? Yes, the price was already arguably low, especially since they had just recently knocked $40,000 off the asking price. But still. In the end, I was only able to negotiate another $5000 off from the final price, though I suspect if he hadn’t been so boisterous, I could have done better.

In the end, it didn’t matter. This was the house, my own little slice of suburban paradise. My offer was quickly accepted. My bank was a breeze to deal with, approving me almost instantly. I could even close in a matter of days if need be. Unfortunately, as motivated as the seller was, the process started moving very slowly indeed and six weeks later, instead of moving in, I was walking through the house with the home inspector.

The second look at the house was a real eye opener. Yes, the love was still there, but it was a more rational, settled-in feeling the second time around. Walking through this time, I was far more conscious of the troubles that lay ahead. The upstairs bathroom went from merely disgusting to total tear out. That will cost some real money, I thought. Great. None of the light fixtures work in here. And was that water damage on the ceiling? I took a picture and got out of there as quickly as possible.

Beyond the bathroom, the pine paneling became the bane of my existence. It was everywhere. The entrance hall was completely consumed by it. The living room had a single facing wall of it, framing the fireplace. Upstairs, the second bedroom was all pine. And with the sloping ceiling Cape Cod houses are known for on the top floor, it gave the whole room a cabin in the woods feeling. Except for the disgusting, stained dusty rose carpeting which immediately pulled your mind from a romantic rustic setting into the kind of harsh reality usually reserved for makeover shows on cable TV.

More bad carpet waited in the other rooms as well. The master bedroom had grey carpet. The living room was powder blue. The previous owners had a nerdy hot nineteen year old son who lived in a cave-like room with almost black walls and a speckled grey shag carpet. His room had that distinctly male smell so associated with young adults, a clever mix of sweat and cum. In my head I debated which would be more difficult: painting those walls a lighter color or getting the smell out.

With the spell of first love broken, I saw the basement with fresh eyes. Yes, the bar I loved was still there. But it was surrounded by falling ceiling tiles, more bad pine paneling and seventeen years of junk. In the corner though, I noticed they had a beautiful old upright piano. Even though I don't play and my singing is worse than my playing. I have always imagined myself the kind of person who sits down at a party in front of the piano and starts playing and singing. In my head, everyone is happy with that scenario although in reality it is more likely that I would be met with a mix of resentment and horror.

When it came to the flaws of the house, the inspector pointed out much of what I could see myself. On the bright side, he noted the steel beams and solid construction of the house. It is true. The bones of the place are that of a war bunker, all steel and concrete. Even the garage is made of cinderblock that goes all the way up through the roof. My house was built at the height of the cold war and designed to withstand a nuclear annihilation in nearby Manhattan. Replace a few blown out windows and a fresh coat of paint and it would be like the apocalypse never happened.

Unfortunately for me, some rooms looked like the apocalypse already had happened. I knew it would take months, possibly years, to erase the decades of heterosexuality that enveloped the house like a virus. But mostly I pondered the seventeen years of crap the previous owners had accumulated. Every closet, every attic nook, every inch of the basement was filled to bursting with dusty boxes and half forgotten mementos. For the first time, I realized truly why the process was taking them so long. How do you begin to pack up two decades of your life?

Having owned a house before, I know the feeling of needing to fill empty spaces. And as I looked around at the four bedrooms and the cavernous basement, I knew my instinct would be to act exactly as they had and just keep filling until full. Already our apartment was as crammed as could be and a storage unit out in Queens overflowed with everything else. True, everything would fit into my new home easily, but that itch to keep going in amassing a fortune of junk was already yearning to be scratched.

As I climbed into my old car and headed back to Manhattan, I was still excited but my excitement was tempered with caution and perhaps a tinge of panic. What had I really gotten myself into? I am a man of grand ideas but little action. It was possible that with this house, I had bitten off more than I could chew, especially in my emotional state. Unfortunately, it was too late. There was nothing in the inspection that would be a dealbreaker and unless I wanted to lose my deposit, this house was going to be mine no matter what.

Vlada Vignettes

Thursday, April 12th. 2:30am. 96th Street Subway platform. iPod on shuffle. Tears well up in my eyes. Oh no. Bruce Vilanch is right. At a certain point, you do start breaking down all the time for no reason, like an old Buick.

Why am I crying? And it's not even crying. It's movie crying: a welling of tears, a trickle out of one eye. That's how I know it's not real. But why the tears? Was it something someone said at the bar tonight?

"You are forty, so who cares what you think."

That can't possibly be it. That was hilarious.

I click to the next song. k.d. lang singing *Big Boned Gal.* I am already welling up. I might as well go full tilt boogie. I search k.d. for her cover of the Patsy Cline classic *Three Cigarettes In An Ashtray.*

"Two cigarettes in an ashtray. My love and I in a small café. Then a stranger came along. Everything went wrong. Now there's three cigarettes in the ashtray."

I saw k.d. lang sing this as the encore at her concert in Reno last year, when Romaine and I were in town for the gay rodeo finals.

Next to seeing Ella Fitzgerald in her final concert at the Hollywood Bowl before they cut off her legs, this is my most treasured concert memory. Suddenly, I am my own grandmother, welling up at Johnny Hodges' sax.

My mind turns to the call with my home insurance lady Mary Anne today. We spent an hour on the phone talking about my new house to determine my coverage and when the questioning turned to possessions, I got very depressed. First item: jewelry. I don't own any and I'm a man and who cares. But then as we went down the list, I realized I don't have anything of value. Some sentimental things, but I own nothing worth keeping when I am gone. I am the only thing I have of value.

Damn, now the song is over. Need to start it again if I am going to maintain this dramatically somber mood.

"I watched him take her from me. Now his love is no longer my own. Now they have gone. I sit alone. And watch one cigarette burn away."

This is good but it doesn't really match the mood I am in. True, I was at a bar tonight with Ben Harvey but Vlada hardly counts as a "small café." And yes, someone did horn in on us, but so what? We're just friends and we were just talking.

I switch to k.d. lang's cover of the *Valley of the Dolls* theme song. I have a remix of it in my iPod that is a better match to the late hour otherworldliness of the subway platform. And earlier our conversation was straight out of the movie (and probably the book, although like most books I can discuss in casual conversation, I have never read it).

Vlada is a vodka bar around the corner from my office, so I tend to haunt it like the TV set in *Poltergeist*. They have a row of infusing jugs along the top of the bar filled with vodkas of every flavor and an icy strip along the bar itself for setting your drink into, although it just reminds me of an old freezer in need of defrosting. Shows how old I am.

I like Vlada because I enjoy a Bloody Mary at all hours of the day or night and the one they make with the pepper vodka is delightful (horseradish, not so much). Until recently they didn't have many drag shows or cabaret acts, which meant you could actually carry on a conversation with friends, always a plus for a chatterbox like me. It's a mixed crowd there, in the sense that it is almost exclusively attractive white gay men but the ages range from twenties right into the very early forties. That is what is known as gay diversity. At every age though, the gays are largely the same (hair, clothes, attitude, all ripped from the pages of the same gay catalog fantasy) and I enjoy watching them in their antics as I try to figure out their stories. I have given up any notion of flirting and really am just one of those people who now visits a bar exclusively to drink, stare at the other patrons bitterly and mutter to himself.

My favorite character to people watch at Vlada is an attractive young attorney named Charlie. I spotted him on one of my adventures there and then kept seeing him. A few short minutes at home later on the stalker's almanac Friendster.com and I had all the background information I needed to launch my investigation. I spend a lot of time speculating about his life, who he is meeting, and what his motivations are. Sometimes he leans in close with the guy he is talking with. Perhaps it is a date, maybe a first date. Other times he is clearly just palling around with friends.

I don't know why Charlie is so interesting to me. Yes, he is very cute and long distance runner thin, but I am not sexually attracted to him in any way. He would need to be blond for me to develop that kind of unhealthy obsession. I think he is so appealing because it seems that he is always there and when he is there, he is always smiling. Obsessively happy people fascinate me because I demand to know why.

Normally, I see Charlie there at Vlada, but this time, Ben Harvey was there. We recently became friends and hanging out tonight he mentioned that he had noticed that I blog about Charlie's nights at Vlada with the kind of dedication usually reserved for anthropologists. Ben Harvey mentioned that they knew each other. By the way, I need to use Ben's full name because he can't be just Ben because the divine Ben Patrick Johnson is just Ben to me. Besides, some people just sound better with their whole names, like my frenemy Dan Renzi. Ben Harvey is one of those people. His full name together is musical, satisfying.

Ben Harvey and I have been emailing for weeks now, since we finally met last month at the God-awful Gay Expo, which I think should be their official name. To make matters worse, there are actually two different gay expos, one in the spring and one in the fall, as if one God-awful one isn't enough they had to get all twinsies on us.

I think he was reluctant to meet me at the event for some reason even though I noticed he had checked out my own Friendster page in the months before our fateful encounter at the Javits Center. Professional curiosity, no doubt. I don't know that I can attribute his reluctance to me specifically because in some ways he seems like a reluctant person. I am also reluctant in public and I sensed that we are alike in that way. Although I know someone who always says to me "guys like us" which invariably is a comparison of how we look and I think I am much cuter than that guy. So at the risk of seeming like that guy and *that* guy, Ben Harvey is more attractive and he and I are just alike in our reticence.

Like me, Ben works in radio, though I would classify him as more of a radio professional. He has a degree from Brown for Christ's sake! I'm just a guy who lucked into a radio show because I was around and willing. There are clear differences between us beyond that, most notably Ben is blond and thin, two aspects that I covet. And even though he is a reluctant figure in public he has a golden radiance that I lack. No wonder he is hosting things for Here TV. He definitely belongs in front of a camera not hiding behind a mike.

Heavenly development though, he got hit on tonight and I was completely ignored. That was delightful. Some people who like being the center of attention (like me), like it all the time. I only like it part time, the way a rich person might dedicate themselves to charity. So when I am not in the mood, I am delighted to retreat into the shadows. With the exception of my roommate Mike, most of my friends are, for lack of a better word, showboaters. Tonight, Ben Harvey was the shimmering light of blond deliciousness and I was the fat friend in the shadows, drinking down the remnants of my thirties like so much melted ice in a cocktail glass. But more on that later.

I made no effort today. I spent hours dealing with the final details of the new house. I cooked dinner at 1pm and socked it away in the fridge for later enjoyment. I barely brushed my hair and wore an eight year old Gap shirt that every gay man in the world owns, just like always. I rolled into work with my winter parka and an air of resignation an hour before the show. Typical. I was all set for a night of TV viewing at home: *Lost*, *Top Design*, *Top Model*. Top ass sitting in a recliner in front of a 50 inch TV. This is what my life typically is.

I already only go out a couple of nights a week, so my impending move to the suburbs will do little to impact my already threadbare social life. But Ben Harvey sent me a text message (txt to the kids out there) but then followed with an email in case I was too old to be a text messenger. Eh. He's right. I am on the cusp. So after the show, out I went to Vlada.

In the bathroom at Vlada wondering why gay men don't know how to flush a urinal, vainly trying to do something with my hair in the mirror, I catch eyes with the gay at the sink next to me.

"It looks good."

Is he talking about my hair or referring to me as a third person object? Either way, it's enough to propel my carcass out of the men's room and return to the gay fray. Ben Harvey and I have long entwined discussions about gay media, radio, dating, and relationships. A few laughs here and there, the biggest when I talk about going to Starbucks the next morning after drinking in gay bars all night and pulling a dirty wad of singles out of my wallet, change from the various twenties I tossed out the night before. "I have to stop stripping." I like to say as I hand the money to the cashier. It's a good line. Maybe I will use it at Phoenix Pride this weekend, although in most parts of the country, you get fives and tens back when you pay for a drink with a twenty. It might not work outside this moment in time.

Then Ben Harvey goes to the bathroom for the 70th time. A man walks past me, but then stops. He has a variation on the worst line in bar history.

"Why aren't you smiling?"

So many good answers: "Because you didn't keep walking." Or "Because you are talking to me right now." I choose "Because I am an alcoholic and my glass is empty." I shake my glass in the air so the ice clinks loudly against the side. He moves on. I have too much baggage for him.

Another man walks over. Will my empty glass and I get no peace tonight? And how long does it take Ben Harvey to pee?

"I am in town from Texas. I have been in New York for four weeks. In all the time I have been here you are the most masculine I guy I have seen."

I want to stifle a girlish giggle. "You are kidding right?"

"No I mean it. You are so masculine. What do you say?"

"Leave now."

He whines. "Most guys at least say 'thank you' when you compliment them."

“Sorry. I meant, you should leave now before I say or do anything so you might still believe that. To be honest, I am just too old and too tired at this hour to wave my hands about wildly.”

I was besieged! And then after Ben Harvey finally returned there was JT and of course John. The third cigarette in the ashtray.

Ben Harvey and I were having a perfectly nice time minding our own business. First we were standing downstairs but Ben Harvey is fragile and needed to sit down. We move upstairs, but then drag sensation Edie, who is talented but loud, starts in on her show and a couple of homos who work in radio can’t hear each other talk because they are both varying degrees of deaf now. It comes with the job.

We move to the seats downstairs and continue our conversation. Suddenly, as exuberant and crazy in love as a Beyonce video, JT gallops into our conversation. He is nice enough, twenty-six and full of enough energy for us both to think he might be taking drugs. But what? Through his succession of ridiculously hot friends, we learn he is a dancer or maybe choreographer. I hear a connection to Britney Spears mentioned (a friend brags that JT came up with one of her signature dance moves) but since she shaved her head and beat a parked car with an umbrella she hardly seems like the kind of reference you want printed in bold on your resume.

JT introduces us to his "famous" best friend John. Famous John is a cutie 25 year old who is as comatose as JT is gregarious. It is almost as though JT is actually sucking the life out of him in the middle of the bar, right before our eyes. Ben Harvey and John hit it off, but Gay Commandment #1: Thou shalt not covet thy homos best friend if thy homo hit on you first, even if thy homo's best friend is way hotter than thy homo and totes into you. So Ben Harvey is polite to JT ping ponging back and forth to our table while trying very hard to covertly signal his interest John who is sitting very still next to him.

In my good ear, I half hear Ben Harvey tell JT that I am his boyfriend. Happy to run easy interference I play my role to the hilt. Of course, I also use this as an opportunity to tease Ben Harvey mercilessly. "My boyfriend *loves* it when guys hit on him. He loves the attention!" Well the attention from JT goes on too long and too dramatically and Ben Harvey wants to leave and even I start longing for a nap. Earlier JT didn't believe I was really 37, but now he is annoyed enough to use it against me. "You are forty, so who cares what you think." His flounce is especially pronounced as he dismisses me like a school bell.

Hmmmaybe, I am the most masculine guy in New York City.

John, who isn't "famous" at all but instead is a very attractive dog washer at Biscuits and Bath, leaves. JT returns to invite us to someone's apartment for a party, but, even though this is how I met Eric one of my greatest friends in the world fifteen years ago, I am far too old now to be attending impromptu parties at strange apartments on a Wednesday. Ben Harvey is right. It is time to call it a night. So I leave Ben Harvey on the corner of 8th Avenue with a promise to write out our evening for posterity. And then decide to take the subway home. I could take a cab, but I want the extra time to really work over the details in my drunken head.

The subway takes forever to arrive and I am ready to climb into bed even before the subway train pulls into my stop at 125th street in Harlem. Tomorrow I will get up early and watch a sea of TV before heading into work. I probably should have stayed home and watched TV tonight but that's what an old person would do. I have decades of that ahead of me, in my house filled with sentimental favorites and nothing of real value, listening to k.d. lang and thinking about the good old days when I saw her in concert and what life was like with record players and before the internet. But tonight I am the only thing I have of value and I chose to release my asset (such as it is) from the vault, to put my cigarette in the ashtray and experience life in the small café that is Manhattan.

Just this once.

The Shaggy B.D.

Wednesday, April 18th. Matty and I have been friends for a long time, the better part of a decade, which is forever in gay years. In a community where you practically get a medal for knowing the name of the guy you slept with last night, being friends for ten plus years is the equivalent of surviving the storming of the beach at Normandy. I love Matty even though there are really two of him, or I should say, there is one but he exists in two different worlds simultaneously. On the one hand, he is the doyen of NYC gay high society, friend of a friend to every hot man on the island of Manhattan. The other world Matty exists in revolves quietly around an intimate cabal of smart, artistically talented friends, men of substance and connections if not always means.

Matty has been unsuccessful at integrated me into either of these worlds since I moved to the city back in 2001, but not for lack of trying. Longing to be part of the latter world and its inner circle of quiet power and dignity, I am most closely suited (which is to say, not at all) to the former. I am the first to admit that I am not an easy person to be friends with. Occasionally hilarious, fiercely loyal, devoted even, but my personality is like the fingers of *Edward Scissorhands:* a ton of fun until you get sliced. And the cuts can run deep, my friend. Ever patient, Matty continues to invite me to party after fundraiser after social function in the hopes that something, anything, will stick.

I dropped by Shag tonight for Matty's official, actual birthday. Shag is a bar just across the Chelsea border in the West Village, notable for its trademark shag carpet wall and narrow length which when crowded (its only speed) gives one the delight of forced sexual harassment at the hands of many attractive young gay men. As is the case with virtually every hip and interesting establishment on the island, Matty is close friends with the owner, manager, bartenders and DJ, along with at least half the patrons. Matt is not tall, but always easy to find in a crowd because he is invariably at the center of it. Endlessly adorable with a personality that says "the party starts here," he is an eternally appealing person. His slim toned torso, an unchanged holdover from his years rowing crew at Notre Dame, is packed tight in a signature Polo shirt, the logo of which consumes the entire left side of his chest and, along with the Great Wall of China, can be seen from space.

Ben Harvey and I conspired to create an A Gay power foursome tonight at Shag. *The Fantastic Four*! But better than the movie. My job was to get us to a place where Matty would be and Ben Harvey would bring Charlie. That was the deal, like a cold war prison exchange in East Berlin. Oh Charlie. I have been studying travels with Charlie, largely at Vlada, my usual watering hole, for months now. Of late, he has not been there, leading me to believe I am a more dedicated alcoholic and not quite the recluse I tend to see myself as. As a modern day Jane Goodall, crouched in the dark recesses of the noisy gay bar, jotting random notes in my head for use later in my online journal of events, I spied Charlie on more than one occasion, though never wanted to interrupt the natural order of things by talking to him. From a distance, he has a winning smile, which is not diminished by closer inspection. Tonight at Shag he reminded me that we had met before, some time ago at Beige.

It is at this point that the trolley really jumped the tracks. For some time now, I have been on the brink of nervous collapse. I have had two different emotions colliding inside me for weeks, like a pair of hurricanes flung together in such a way that neither has an eye of calm anymore. On the one hand, I have my prolonged house closing, the stress of which has ruined my normally blissful slumber for three weeks. The second storm was caused by the Bravo series *Work Out*, which is especially infuriating because it is neither a show that I like nor one I watch!

I watched the first season with mild interest because I am willing to give any show with hot shirtless men a chance. The whole endeavor is as phony as anything in the "reality" canon and the fact that it is overwhelmed by gays and lesbians fails to spark any interest for me beyond wondering when we get to see some hot man disrobing next. Before this current season began airing, one of the participants, a personal trainer named Doug, died in real life. This is always a horrible occurrence but certainly no reason to stop the cameras from rolling!

I caught the season opener and seeing Doug alive, blissfully unaware of his impending death (promised a few episodes later) has hit me very hard. In particular, the “fat” trainer Jesse, who is the love of my life, showed callous disregard for Doug. “I don't need him in my life,” he casually declared, no doubt hoping for and cementing his guaranteed camera time. In hindsight, such blithe muggings for extra airtime on a basic cable channel look shallower than a child's wading pool and just as disgusting to watch as a soggy, full diaper floating in it.

Faced with Doug's mortality, I have been spurred into action, not to let that kind of pettiness rule my life. In an effort to tie up my own loose ends (just in case) I even decided to finally make some kind of peace with my ex-boyfriend known forever as Fat Ass. For years I had been playing a game of reconciliation with him. People like Fat Ass who are constant and habitual liars tend to lose their sense of any reality, especially with the people they have spent so much time lying to. The world of denial they live in is so huge that it is easy for those on the outside who are aware of what is going on to manipulate it to their own advantage.

Every few months, he would contact me and say he wanted to bury the hatchet. I knew of course that if I threw it back at him that I didn't want to because he is a liar who ruined my life for a good chunk of time, he could just feel justified in blaming me for, well, everything. "I tried," he could tell himself with some satisfaction. And go on with his life with a clear conscience. So instead, I would respond, "Yes, let's get together!" putting the ball back in his court, knowing full well that he had no intention of doing any such thing and I would not hear from him again until the whole process repeated itself a few months later. This game of cat and mouse went on for years.

Doug's death fueled my endgame with Fat Ass and made me realize that such childish shenanigans didn't serve anyone, least of all me. So I made a firm date to meet him for coffee at a local Starbucks. We had a perfectly amicable discussion about absolutely nothing for more than an hour. No apologies or discussions of the past. Just polite chit chat. We both left and went our separate ways and I have not seen or heard from him since. Mission accomplished.

It also helped confirm my impulsive decision to buy my house, spend more time with my friends and in general, has left me with a constant sense of urgency about things said and done. It has made me more accomplished, and also more scattered in my thoughts, as I sift through the sands of my life, looking for the shards of broken glass to throw out. Compounding this with the Byzantine rules surrounding home purchase in the state of New York and I can hardly remember my own name. So tonight when, after four hours of radio and sitting on an empty stomach and a full drink, Charlie mentioned Beige, I couldn't for the life of me remember the bar or its location in New York City, even though I have been there at least 20 times in the last six years. This gave Charlie the upper hand to chide me for the rest of the evening about my inability to remember who or what I was. These kids today.

I did my radio show with Cyd Zeigler as guest host today since Romaine, suffering through a pregnancy that feels as long as an elephant's gestation, had the night off. Cyd and I became friends in 2003 when we first launched the radio show and we wanted someone to come on the air to talk about sports every once in a while. I had never met him but I knew about his site OutSports.com that he co-founded and told Romaine, "We should have the cute one on the show." It turns out I am just as shallow on the radio as I am in real life and in my choice of TV shows.

I always feel guilty asking someone to host the show with me and then abandoning them the second the show is over, like a selfish sex partner (although weirdly my true reputation as a selfish sex partner is well established). So, I cajoled Cyd into joining me for a drink at Shag and turned our Fantastic Four into a Fabulous Five. The main reason for our gathering was for Ben to finally formally be introduced to Matty. They knew of each other but didn't know each other, so tonight was a real opportunity for them to get to meet. The whole thing seems positively old-fashioned in our era of sex tapes as

PR stunt and nauseatingly candid reality shows. But people should actually know each other instead of forming wild opinions from a distance. This is what made Ben Harvey bringing Charlie along so important. Now we could both meet someone we knew of but didn't already really know.

Charlie took an instant liking to Cyd, hanging on his every word. Cyd told the incredibly endearing and romantic story about how he and his boyfriend Dan met and how patiently Cyd waited for years for the two of them to get together. It was like a gay Hallmark Hall of Fame movie where by the end credits it was clear to anyone watching that there was no daylight between them. Much to my amusement, when Cyd got up to use the bathroom, Charlie turned to me, a sparkle in his eye, "He's so great. I have to get his number." Were we even listening to the same story?

Even though we all spent hours jammed together tightly at a table, my back perpetually up against the shag wall, I barely got a chance to talk to Ben Harvey, or Matt, or even Cyd, who I dragged out on a school night. The conversations were flying fast and furious at the table and I ping ponged my way between the two, never really connecting to either one. Funny that I turned into a fifth wheel at a meeting of my own making, but that really is how I prefer it. I got to spend time with some of my favorite people and even make a new friend. And since it is important to learn from every experience, I did get two things from this evening just by sitting there listening and looking.

First, the gays sure do like to worry. And sometimes they worry about things that mean absolutely nothing at all. Maybe we just like to worry for worrying's sake. Maybe it's a misplaced maternal instinct that, lacking anything to mother, we endlessly mother ourselves and each other. Doug's death has reminded me that it just isn't worth worrying about, whatever it is.

Second, I learned that even if I can't remember my own name, or a bar I got drunk in with Matt in Los Angeles (Cherry) or a bar I got drunk in with Matt and Charlie in New York (Beige), or the name of the guy who wrote about me in the New York Times in June 2003 (Bob Morris), I never forget to be an ass about grammar. By Manhattan standards, I may have a fourth grade education, but when Ben's sweet, sweet friend Jeremy, who writes for the New York Times wandered over to our table and said "when Saddam was hung," I reflexively muttered "hanged" under my breath. Twice.

Because just like life, once just isn't enough to say everything you need to say.

May Day!

Tuesday, May 29th – The house closed on my mother's birthday (May 9th) and Mike and I moved in over this past Memorial Day weekend. The timing of the move was all part of an intensely coordinated plan built around not missing any of our favorite TV shows. After all, when you are in the midst of the May season finales, the last thing you want is to be without TV when the end comes. And I am not ashamed to admit that I have an unhealthy attachment to watching television. Hello. My name is Derek and I am a watchaholic.

Memorial Day weekend was obviously the easiest weekend for the move. It was the last weekend of the month, meaning we would be cleared out of our apartment in plenty of time for the new tenants to move in on the first of June. In fact, we would be all gone and cleaned out by Saturday giving them a few extra days to get in. Our landlady Evora had rented out our old place to two very nice young women, fresh out of college, making their way in the big city. We met them and thought they were charming. They were just the kinds of tenants we hoped would replace us. Although, I suppose we should have warned them that in the past, Evora would occasionally forget her keys and call us to let her back into the building. But I guess some things are better discovered on your own.

The movers of course wanted to schedule the move for the middle of the week when they were considerably less busy, but our biggest issue was with the TV. The last of the season finales was airing on Thursday, the date of our move. So we had to be very careful about the timing of turning cable on and over so we wouldn't miss anything.

I had a bunch of stuff already in my storage unit out in Queens that needed to be moved to the house anyway. So, I decided to rent a truck and move that stuff in first. That would give us some mattresses and bedding and most important TVs that we could have at the house before we arrived. That way, we could have the cable switched on there a couple of days early so we could begin recording shows up there that would be overlap to keep us from missing anything. I thought it was a very smart plan and it went off without a hitch.

The week before the big move, I loaded up a rental truck in Queens and headed up to the new house. It has been noted on many occasions, not the least of which by my own mother, that I am not a very good driver. So it shouldn't have been much of a surprise that as I rounded the corner near the cemetery in Sleepy Hollow, that I accidentally went up onto the curb a bit and nearly tipped the truck over. For an instant, the image of the truck on its side, split open like a full Jiffy Pop pan, furniture tumbling out like so much hot popcorn, flashed through my mind. But the truck rolled off the small curb just as quickly as it had jumped onto it and I safely made my way back up to the house.

As I have done frequently, I got a bit lost along the way. When I first moved to NYC, the biggest thing I missed about LA was going to the supermarket, pushing your cart up to the car, loading your groceries in the back and driving away like a human being. In Manhattan, you can only eat what you can carry. Think about that for a minute. If you want to know why New Yorkers are so thin, it isn't just all the walking. For your next diet, only buy what you can actually carry without a shopping cart. You will find yourself making hard choices and buying and eating a lot less, and going to the grocery store four times a week.

So, wanting to live in New York without actually living like someone who did, I would drive out to New Jersey just across the bridge for the sole purpose of buying food and liquor. What I discovered in the alternate universe that is New Jersey is that road signs don't make any sense. It takes only an instant to become hopelessly and horrendously lost.

On one trip, we were headed back to the city and we passed a small motel you could see the Empire State Building from. I thought it was silly that people would stay so close to the city but not actually stay in the city. But then, after driving around lost for the better part of an hour, passing that same damned motel for the third time, I realized that I probably wasn't the first person in history who started to think, "Perhaps we should just make camp here and make a second try at dawn."

The roads of Westchester County where my new house allegedly existed are no less mystifying. My roommate Mike is convinced that the streets are named and designed solely for people who grew up there and are actually meant to dissuade strangers from visiting or staying. I got lost the first time we drove up to meet the realtor, the first time I drove to the house for the inspection and once again in an unwieldy moving van.

The source of the problem is the number nine. There is Route 9 and then there is Route 9A. And sometimes they are together and sometimes they are not. Knowing which one you are on is vitally important. And knowing when to jump onto 9A from any of the highways that run parallel to it is the difference between a thirty minute trip and a whole afternoon.

Naturally, I had it in my head that I could rent a truck, fill it with all of the things in my storage unit, drive it to the new house, unload it, drive back to the truck rental location and still get to the studio in time for the show at six. As I drove through the wilds of Westchester that prospect began to seriously dim. Fortunately, I have no concerns for the condition of my furniture or the dignity with which it should arrive. Therefore, the contents of my storage unit ended up being dumped as unceremoniously as possible through the first available door before speeding off like Thelma and Louise trying for Mexico.

Fortunately, the movers were more careful with the rest of our furniture. After the Oscar party, I began wrapping all of my delicate midcentury wood furniture in protective plastic wrap. By the end of April, my dining room looked like some kind of obsessive Tupperware party gone horribly awry. As it was, I had designated the dining room the "staging area" for the move where, as we packed boxes, we would stack them all neatly. All of the boxes were clearly labeled with which of the rooms in the new house they needed to go into. And to be helpful, and possibly insane, I created diagrams of the house on 11x14 paper with the rooms clearly marked so there would be no doubt for the movers what should go where.

I am not normally this organized, that is my roommate Mike's job. His many years in the Army I began to discover weren't so much an influence on his behavior as a dream fulfilled. He is, by nature, an Army man: organized, neat and detailed. The Army merely reinforced his world view about an urgent need for order in a chaotic world. Perhaps I thought some of it had rubbed off on me, but really I think it was just all my pent up frustration at not being in the new house yet that caused me to so aggressively rearrange the deck chairs on the Titanic that was the Harlem apartment. I am not control, I am chaos.

And so we spent the long weekend unpacking, but mostly we spent it cleaning. Having already given the house a thorough cleaning once, it became immediately necessary, especially when Mike arrived, to do it again. When we left the Harlem apartment, it was nearly as immaculate as when we moved in to it, brand new in December 2002. I steam cleaned all the carpets and every surface was scrubbed down to a polish. Even Randy's Jello-O shot was very nearly faded to a complete obscurity. As we left, Evora marveled that it looked like no one had ever lived there which I think Mike took particular pride in.

But no sooner had I put the last of the cleaning supplies in the back of my little convertible, that I was unloading them into the new house to repeat the process again. Despite finding a supermarket's worth of supplies under the sink, some parts of the house looked like they hadn't been cleaned in years, maybe decades. And clearly near the end of their own move, the previous owners just gave up. Decades of accumulated crap were still stacked high and deep in the basement. But there in a dusty, dank corner of the basement was the upright piano that I had coveted during my first visit to the house. And as we settled in to watch our last few shows in the new house, delivery pizza in hand, I suddenly found myself ready for the task at hand. I found calm and peace amid the chaos. Everything was going to work out just fine.

June Bug

Thursday, June 28th - Everything is settled into the house now and so begins the real fun. In the midst of unpacking, we took the first of what I assume will be a million trips to the local Home Depot. The first order of gay business: new switch plates for the lights in the house. In a fixer-upper situation, this might not seem like a top priority but you didn't see these switch plates! The previous owners had a penchant for what can only be described as overly adorable decorative plates. Teddy bears and hearts jut out of them at every turn, even in rooms clearly designated for adults. It was just too much for my gay eyes to bear and they were the first things to go.

But the real nightmare was a lone shelf in the kitchen. Mike and I decided early on that the basement would be home base for our TV viewing, which means it is nothing less than the center of our universe. I liked the idea of a living room without a TV and with so much space we had the luxury of turning the basement into our fantasy rumpus room. The only real issue with spending so much time in the basement is the narrow entrance from the kitchen above. As it turns out, the door to the basement stairs is hidden around a small corner basically behind the refrigerator. So now this is our new pinch point. Despite three floors and thousands of square feet, my roommate Mike and I are constantly running into each other at the fridge. And complicating matters is that shelf.

Long, wooden with three hearts carved into the base, it pokes out of the wall at eye level beginning right at the corner of the wall leading to the basement. To make matters worse, it is painted the same color as the wall, camouflaging it from easy view. In our first few days, both of us walked into it about fifty times. At the risk of our new neighbors thinking we are in some kind of fight club, something had to be done. One too many bangs and that was it for Mike. He grabbed the tool box and started tearing at the shelf with everything he could find. Yes, he did gouge a fairly noticeable hole in the wall where one of the impossible screws had been, but neither of us cared once the shelf was out. Holes can't hit you! In addition, the previous owners had painted around the shelf, so its removal left behind three perfect hearts painted into a pink patch of wall where the shelf had been, but it didn't matter. It was already an improvement. The fridge continues to be a pinch point, but at least it isn't dangerous anymore.

That is the beauty of owning a house. If you don't like something, you can change it. The downside is that if something doesn't work, there is no one else responsible for fixing it but you. The house came as is which it turns out meant the burners on the stove didn't work. How people could live without a working stovetop is beyond me, but the first big chunk of money spent had to go toward buying a new stove. Naturally Mike, who has the uncanny knack of always liking what turns out to be the most expensive version of whatever you need to buy, wanted to buy a high end, shiny stainless steel stove. Never mind that it didn't match any of the other cream-colored appliances, stainless was all he liked.

Mike and I don't share the same taste. I am a midcentury gay in my midcentury and have loved the period since before it rushed back into fashion recently. Mike on the other hand would live in a concrete block infused with nothing but glass and steel, all surfaces free of clutter and as shiny as the sun. Alexis Stewart, who is Mike's doppelganger when it comes to interior style, considered it the highest compliment when someone came over to her apartment and said that it looked like no one lived there.

I think if he had his way he would live in one of those model homes of the future with drawers that disappear into walls and walls that fold away like origami. Unfortunately, already knowing how much a house costs to maintain, I knew that spending twice as much on a basic appliance is nothing but a waste of money that will be needed later when a staircase collapses or the chimney falls away from the house.

The first time I bought a house back in 1999, I didn't know what to do or expect. I spent a great deal of time thinking about what I wanted to do but very little time actually doing anything.

Eventually over a four year period, I managed to paint some walls, replace a few light fixtures and poorly repair a single step. It was not exactly the kind of gay makeover that cable TV channels are built around. Having Mike as a roommate has made such lazy dreaming impossible. Mike is a man of action.

All month Mike has been prodding me to buy things and get things done. When are you taking up that carpet in the living room? When are we painting that wall? How quickly can we rip that light fixture out of the ceiling and burn it in the yard? So many questions, so much to do! But with TV wrapped up for the summer, we did have a lot of free time on our hands.

Not interested in waiting on me, Mike immediately set about transforming his room. Mike took a room on the first floor of the house, while I am upstairs in the cape. He decided on a decorating theme that I will describe here as what would have happened if the Japanese had won the war. The room was yellow with red trim and he found a ceiling fan online that looked like the propeller of a 1940s fighter plane. It looked like the bed was about to be subjected to a kamikaze raid and I wouldn't have been at all surprised if he fashioned his bed into the shape of a battleship. But Mike was going for a vague scheme not the story clarity of a line queue at Tokyo Disneyland, so it was more subtle than that.

The rest of the alterations in the house have started to emanate out from Mike's room like a shockwave. I have been trying to remove the wallpaper in the hallway upstairs but there is a second layer of even older wallpaper underneath it and oh look, I see something shiny and distracting! Meanwhile, Mike is more aggressive about getting the two of us to remove the wallpaper in the downstairs hallway and naturally his urging is making quick work of that project.

Even though we have a different sensibility when it comes to interior design, in the sense that he has one, I do defer to him in one area. Mike has many fine qualities but probably his best quality is when it comes to color. Me who drove my poor mother to the point of surrender trying to match the giraffe to the lion in Garanimals am no help when it comes to design. But Mike has a real eye for color and he likes to make bold choices.

Now because he is ultra modern and I like midcentury, we do not always see eye to eye. I want to stay true to the narrow color scheme of traditional Cape Cod houses (variations on blue and green) and Mike has come to grudgingly respect those boundaries when choosing colors for the public rooms of the house. The guest room next to his has midnight blue walls and seriously the most unappetizing grey speckled carpet you have ever seen. So, getting the walls to the pale green he picked out will be no small feat. But Mike has been researching primers online and he thinks we can do it.

I have to be honest. I do appreciate Mike's prodding. If he wasn't around, it is a certainty that the level of dirt and disrepair I found the house in would only lead me to a life straight out of Grey Gardens that much sooner. Yes, some people question why we continue to be roommates after all these years absent a romantic entanglement that never was nor never will be. But the truth is, I need Mike. He is like that voice in your head that makes you feel guilty about things left undone but instead of being a voice you can ignore, he is a person standing in front of you in a hallway on a Saturday morning when all you want is a cup of coffee and to sit for the next two days.

And being so active sprucing things up inside the house and digging around in the dirt in the yard to plant things is actually fun. I look forward to weekends at home now so we can set about filling a dumpster full of the previous owner's crap or taping around a windowsill in preparation for painting. But where I had imagined we would be traveling into the city on Saturday nights to party like always, we are often too tired to deal with the long train ride there and back. It is just as easy to go to a movie at our local mall where there are never any other moviegoers and then head home.

I suppose when we got caught up in the excitement of having our own bathrooms and the other advantages to living in the new house, we didn't really think of the ramifications of moving so far out of the city. Yes the commute would be long. At an hour, it was twice our old commute in the city. But the biggest impact has ended up being on our social lives. I didn't factor in the weekends! What of all the bar hopping and movie going on Friday, Saturday and Sunday? Our midweek adventures have been curtailed as well. I am still going out only a night or two during the week so that hadn't really changed, but the last train out of the city is at 1:50am which means no more 3am bar crawls. When it is time to go, we have to go. And that always eats into the fun.

I don't mind so much since even before moving so far away, my own sparse nightlife adventures had not always ended well. We hadn't exactly been party animals before but these new restrictions will take some getting used to. In order to keep ourselves out there socially, this house and our own reluctance to leave it are going to be our biggest challenge to overcome. Getting older and living so far away is a crippling death blow on the party scene. So as much as I love the quiet and the solitude, we are going to have to leave the paint brushes and peeling wallpaper behind every once in a while and take a swing through the urban jungle. But first, we just need to make a quick trip to the Home Depot.

And Baby Makes Three

Saturday, July 21st – The news arrived by text. I guess that is how we do things now. My co-host Romaine had her baby and suddenly the whole world has changed. Romaine doesn't think anything will change but of course it will. How can it not? Four years ago when I met her, she was a skinny party girl living on a single bed in her brother's living room, living on vodka cocktails and late night slices of pizza. Now she is a homeowner with a wife and baby. That's how it is with change. Sometimes, no matter how dramatic, it occurs so slowly it is easy to miss it happening until well into a complete transformation.

In some ways, the life choices Romaine makes are none of my business. The listeners, responding to our on-air chemistry, seem to think we are practically married to each other and not merely co-workers sharing an office. Yes, our relationship goes deeper than office mates, but on the other extreme, the persistent rumor among the listeners that I am the father of her baby is nothing short of insane. Can't they see the murky middle ground we really exist in together? But I suppose that is what they want to believe, like the people who used to watch *Will & Grace* and wondered when those two crazy kids would finally end up together.

I'll admit it is difficult to simultaneously disabuse people of the ridiculous notion that Romaine and I have merged into a single entity and tell the story of how truly intimate our working relationship is but that is the delicate nature of our business. I have had a lot of jobs in my lifetime and been close to many of my co-workers but nothing has been as truly boundary-busting as hosting a daily radio show with another person. Even my many internet years working with (and even living with for a time) my friend Eric, couldn't match the mass consumption of time and space Romaine and I have shared.

First of all, we spend nearly a quarter of our lives together, and most of it is us just talking to each other about our lives. We are a completely united front at the office to the peril of those around us and we do everything together, like psychotic twins. So one of us having a baby is going to have ramifications in the life of the other, however unintentional. It probably explains why Romaine was so reluctant to tell me that she was going to have a baby or even how actively she was trying to get pregnant.

Since I first met her, Romaine has made no secret of her master plan. She wanted to buy a house and have the first of several kids before the age of thirty. Of course, that spring night in 2003 when we first hung out in front of the fireplace at The Park, it never occurred to either of us that we would still be working together when that plan kicked into full gear. So it isn't like I wasn't warned.

But it was still something of a surprise when Romaine told me she was pregnant around Thanksgiving last year.

She hadn't even told me she was trying, even though she had several opportunities to do so. For instance, I had booked us to speak and appear at the gay conference in Washington DC last October and as the date neared, the weekend trip ended up coinciding with her first attempt at insemination. She didn't tell me why, but at the time, she was somewhat agitated about taking the trip and asked lots of questions of what time they needed us down there on that Friday.

This was not completely unusual because with our heavy travel schedule all year promoting ourselves shamelessly at pride events all over the country, both of us would often become weary of living out of a suitcase by the time October rolled around. So Romaine could have told me then what was going on, and even stayed behind from the event to have her doctor's appointment. But instead, she had the appointment a day early and joined me down in DC for the conference. As it turns out, she got pregnant through that first appointment and doing it a day early probably contributed to her having a girl; since female sperm are slower swimmers but live longer. Being inseminated a day early meant there were probably fewer male sperm around to fertilize her egg once it finally arrived a day later at the prime location.

Three weeks later, we were off to another event, this time the Gay Rodeo in Reno, NV. Of all the trips we have taken together over the years, this would probably be our favorite so far. We saw k d lang in concert, bowled a few frames in the alley at our hotel and spent the afternoon with the girls at the bunny ranch. The McRib was back at McDonald's and I was eating them two at a time. And during the rodeo, we sat close together on the bleachers to keep warm while we sipped hot chocolate and cheered for the contestants in the goat dressing event. I guess you kind of have to know us to really understand how ideal that is for us as weekends go but it was really wonderful. Truly transcendently happy moments between the two of us are rare and that weekend was a blissful exception to the drudgery of everyday life.

Right before leaving, Romaine had done an early home pregnancy test and, getting a positive result, did it two more times just to make sure. She could have told me that weekend in Reno, during any of the great quiet moments we shared together, or on the long car ride out to the bunny ranch. Perhaps when we were on the bar crawl bus, she could have explained why she kept refusing the Jell-O shots they kept passing around. But for her own reasons, she kept the news to herself and being the oblivious narcissist that I am; I just consumed her Jell-O shots too and had a great time.

I suppose in a way that will be the last weekend we will ever have together like that. With her pregnancy and maternity leave, she has already had to bail on most of our scheduled pride event appearances out of town. The big test will come in September when we return to Dallas for their pride weekend and Romaine will have to leave her new baby at home for the first time. I am sure she will go no matter what. She is determined like that. In fact, I don't think I know anyone as laser-focused on what she wants as Romaine. After all, she managed to get pregnant on her exact desired timetable, right down to timing the pregnancy so she could still attend her two favorite out of town events: Phoenix in April and Dallas in September.

Maybe it is envy I feel as I look down at her text message, arriving as it did moments before the start of Friday's show. It is all so real and once again Romaine has lapped me in the game of life. I like to think we are so united at work because our goals for ourselves outside the office are so similar. Like Romaine, I also wanted to buy a house before I was thirty, which I did. But Romaine managed to put out a book first which has so long been on my to-do list I can't remember a time not wanting to do it. And now she has a baby, another life goal of mine that her accomplishment makes feel as remote for me as the moon.

I suppose it is never really too late for a man to have a baby. Hollywood is filled with celebrity dads who sired offspring well past their expiration date. But the reality is that the longer I wait, the less and less likely it is. So as I face the daunting emotional spiral of gay middle age rambling around inside a big empty house, I have to ask myself: is what I have enough? Gay men coming of age in the era of AIDS rarely envisioned facing down forty, let alone the contents of a diaper bag. If they thought of strollers, it was guys walking slowly past their West Hollywood apartments late at night, not something that needed to be folded up and gate checked when you board a plane to visit in-laws.

My thoughts turn back to the rodeo in Reno, and the two of us huddled close together on the bleachers, the smell of horse thick in the air. "Remind you of home?" I teased Romaine, prodding her memories of a life raised in the quiet desolation of Wyoming. But the wide open west isn't home anymore, for either of us. We have both staked our claims out on the East coast. And for better or for worse, we are united as man and woman in an often uncivil union. Of course things have changed, and how could they not after so many years, but our destinies are entwined and who knows what the future will bring.

All The Beige

Tuesday, August 14th. It seems impossible to me that it has been months since I have been truly out on the town. But then again, it seemed impossible while hanging out at Shag with Charlie back in April that I couldn't remember in that moment the bar night Beige. We live in impossible times. Romaine is still out on her maternity leave and, while things have been moving very smoothly at the office, it has been a stressful juggling act, like switching from pins to chainsaws. My natural reluctance at going out on the town has found a cozy home in the excuse of Romaine's absence, but enough is enough. I need to be out among people again.

A Tuesday night staple as long as I have been in Manhattan, and dating back well past that into the 90s, Beige, the notorious weekly cluster of hot young gays at Bowery Bar, shows no sign of abating even as simultaneously I seem to be falling by the wayside. I launched a failed club night called REMOTE at a bar around the corner on Tuesday nights in 2001. The club we hosted it in doesn't even exist anymore, but Beige at Bowery Bar lives on.

Bowery Bar is primarily a restaurant with a large patio for outdoor seating. As dinner winds down every Tuesday night, the massive space transforms into a very large bar lounge. It quickly fills with the hottest gay men in the tightest shirts in town. There is frequently a line outside and it isn't just for show. The place gets packed. They can also be very strict about the gayness of the party as well. My friend Tony witnessed a straight couple refused entrance once. "He's bi!" the woman pleaded in reference to her boyfriend. "Not bi enough," was the doorman's retort as he waved them away.

Beige is not my favorite club night or crowd but it is the one that almost everyone agrees on. Tuesdays and Thursdays are the prime nights for socializing in New York City. After resting up from your weekend on Monday, the itch to return to the nightlife returns like clockwork on Tuesday. And Thursday is the kick off to the weekend, especially during the summer when so many weekends are spent out of town. So Beige remains popular and while I was still dealing with my house it was one of the few places I frequented with any regularity through the early summer. Plus, with a looming housewarming party, it was important to re-establish myself in NY gay society and perhaps even make some new friends.

It was a typical Tuesday night at Bowery Bar, although the tides were shifting quickly and the characters drifted past me at a quickened pace all night long. And it all started with Ben Harvey. As often happens, I wasn't just going out to drink. I had a mission. My friendship with Ben Harvey was getting a bit tattered around the edges since our nascent acquaintance begun in February turned out to be built substantially around Rosie O'Donnell's incendiary point of *View*. I didn't realize *how much* it depended on Rosie until she left the show and took our frequent email banter with her. It wasn't just the house that tore me away from my friends. In this case, it was also the end of a shared piece of popular culture. So in an effort to kick-start things, we agreed to a night out on the town at Bowery Bar.

Aside from Rosie, Ben Harvey agrees with me about B-Bar, as it is affectionately referred to. For most young gay men in NYC, it is a haunted house filled with the ghosts of relationships past. Personally, I hadn't had this problem before but for my younger and more attractive friends, it was an issue. So even though it was the weekly "it" destination, the shared feelings for many was at best ambivalence.

I tried to drag some other friends along too, to help create a friendly buffer to the onslaught of swirling gay drama we were no doubt to experience. Sent text messages to my roommate Mike (no response) and Matty, who wanted to know who else was going. I guess I am not as much of a draw as I used to be. Apparently now our friendship needs to come with a solid supporting cast of known players and possibly a gift certificate. Tried to drag muscle-bound gay porn stud Erik Rhodes and his boyfriend Danny out, but the boyfriend was too tired. Given that he is almost half my age, it makes me wonder what is up with these kids today! They all need a little what for!

So I get to Bowery Bar and then I stand in line, like always. No one in Manhattan listens to my radio show (except Ben Harvey) and so I am not what I would call famous. I'm not even a local celebrity. News anchors are local celebrities. Britney Spears is genuinely famous. I am just a person who can't dress himself who works in midtown Manhattan. So I wait in line.

When I get inside, Ben Harvey is standing there with three people. Charlie, who I have studied from afar and now have started to know up close, is the only one I have met or even seen before. The other two say their names but, being deaf from working in radio and also being bad with remembering important things like names; they are lost to the ether before they even open their mouths. It would be exceedingly rude but I almost feel like waving them a "don't bother" gesture when they start to tell me their names because there is just no point to it anyway.

Charlie is cute as always. Thin. I think he was a wearing a sweater even though it's August. He was definitely carrying a book, the title of which was eerily as unmemorable as the names of his friends. Apparently, Charlie has a long commute too so he needs the book and it is quite the conversation starter if you think "what are you reading" is a conversation starter. I suggested he start carrying *Travels with Charlie* which would both start a conversation and make remembering his name a world easier.

Like the ten other people who read my occasionally updated blog, Charlie was disappointed that it wasn't more frequent than a semi-annually white sale. Which reminds me: is celebrating Lincoln's birthday with a white sale weird to anyone but me? Charlie's favorite thing about my blog (aside from my writing about him) is that I link to random Friendster profiles, including his, to prove my point. I am not really sure what the point is. Perhaps it is just me being cute with the three dimensional structure of the internet and linking off to a site filled with photos and other personal information to augment my own limited skills as a storyteller. Choose your own gay adventure.

Off we go, pressing our way through the tightly wound crowd of gays to secure our first drink of the night. Charlie acknowledges the hot bartender in the Boston band tour t-shirt. "Straight but he has gay cheekbones" says Charlie before he is almost immediately besieged by Kyle (attractive in an exclusively gay way), Chris (attractive in any context) and Brand X friend whose name was both unheard and unimportant. You might as well forget at this point that he was even there. I did.

All our drinks in hand, we wander out to the patio. It's a beautiful warm night and the place is filled with beautiful chilly gays. Attractive Chris tried to pull up a chair and then got flummoxed that no one else seemed to be sitting. He probably did legs at the gym today not realizing that all anyone does in a gay bar is stand. He should save his leg routine for a night when he isn't going out drinking. You do arms on a drinking night so you have a nice party pump to fill out your t-shirt. Plus you will drink less if your arms are tired. Ah but he is young and still learning.

He did notice how cute Charlie was but his friend Kyle seemed to be working Charlie pretty hard, like Martha Stewart kneading dough after a rough day at the office, so he kept a respectable, yet longing distance. Clearly I was still studying Charlie and the fascinating world he lives in, though Chris sitting and standing and sitting and standing every few seconds was distracting. As quickly as they appeared, they decamped and beat a hasty retreat to the interior of Beige never to be seen again. Maybe Kyle remembered that he has a boyfriend at home, or perhaps Chris' jack-in-the-box routine was getting to him. I know it was getting to me.

Moments later, none of us were surprised to see Conor, even I who had only met him once before, since we all knew Beige and its cluster fuck of pretty young things was his center of gravity. Conor had previously dated Ben Harvey and then some time later, Matty. This is how Matty and Ben knew of each other, though they had never met, and why I helped bring them together at Shag back in April. All they needed was a meddling, nosey someone in between to arrange a meeting, which I am glad I did. It turned out that Matty and Ben had more going on between them as friends than either of them had with Conor as boyfriends. Things had ended with Matty recently and more amicably than they had ended with Ben. But Ben was very polite when Conor spontaneously joined us on the patio.

I think my initial impression of Conor last time was all wrong, but I think it's because Matty was there with him. This was many months ago when they were still a couple. Where I saw him in the past as "calm and patient and lovely," this time I experienced him outside the looming shadow of Matty and me likey! Me likey very much! The whole time he reminded me of my friend Paul in LA which made me happy and sad at the same time. Like when a cab takes me past my late Great Aunt Caroline's old apartment on West End Avenue and I smile because I remember all the great times there and then cry because she's gone and I can't just pick up the phone and hear her grande dame 1930s movie voice blaring across the line with a volume equal to her deafness.

I forgot to mention how thin Conor looked too. That's very important. He doesn't have the natural reedy slenderness of, say, a Ben Harvey, so being called "thin" is a high compliment indeed. At one point we were plunged into a controversy about being called "thin" instead of "buff" as if being called either one was a bad thing. Conor liked that I said he looked "thin" but Ben Harvey had a definite preference for being "buff" instead of "thin." I am rarely (also known as never) called either one so I am fairly certain that any similar compliment would either win me over instantly or earn my deepest suspicions.

Despite his new thinness, Conor mentioned that he was in the thick of a man drought, which was somewhat the opposite of Charlie's previously announced man strike. Where Charlie had decided to swear off men for a period of time to concentrate on himself, his life this summer and that heavy book he was carrying, Conor wanted to swing from one man to another like a monkey on a tree. So, a few days (or even weeks) without a man and suddenly it is a man drought, and Beige is the very definition of water, water everyone and nary a drop to drink. But just as he said that... a cute guy walked by and looked Conor up and down. "He thinks you are cute." I said pointing at the stranger so blatantly that it prompted him to come over and introduce himself.

Dan. I wasn't sure I heard it correctly in the noisy bar. He leaned in and spelled it out with a smile, his steely blue eyes twinkling. D-A-N, just like in that Annette Bening movie *Being Julia* I love so much. And his friend Tony. T-O-N-Y. He had a third friend with him but the name wasn't spelled out for me, so like so many men tonight he also didn't get heard or remembered. Or maybe it's just me, and I can only remember as many as two names at a time. And to think I was so good at the electronic memory game Simon as a kid. Maybe that is because each color is different and every gay man is exactly the same.

D-A-N initially thought he had run into Conor on Fire Island over the weekend, which is why he had looked him up and down in the first place. Conor assured him that was both unlikely and impossible. Conor and D-A-N made an attempt at small talk but the two of them had all the chemistry of airborne asbestos and a set of lungs. But he did seem to have an eye for Ben Harvey, who was also in something of a man drought I guess, so I kept talking to D-A-N in the hopes that perhaps my feverish matchmaking skills might coalesce for him and B-E-N. No such luck.

The rest of the evening flew by rapidly. Conor turned out to be a fantastic banter partner. And I always love talking to Ben Harvey. In the process of trying to make magic happen between the two three-letter men, I learned that D-A-N was an accountant with Deloitte, liked diet coke but was willing to drink red wine when his friends bought it for him, enjoys big logo Polo shirts (like Matty), pedicures and facials, spent six years in Japan, is independent and financially secure, had friends visiting from the UK and worked a summer as a waiter out on Fire Island. Finding him hours later on Friendster with that kind of information took split seconds. He learned that my name was Derek (which I had to repeat for him later when he forgot it) and that I worked at Sirius. So basically I am a total stranger to him still, even after two hours of conversation.

Suddenly, it was time for me to leave. Since moving to the suburbs, I have learned that the final drunk train home leaves with or without you on it. I made my good-byes and headed off to Grand Central Station. On the train I ended up in the ad hoc queer section with the lone homo (there are *never* homos on the train) who got off early and a tranny reading *A Passage To India* with her party make-up making it's emotionally exhausted journey down her face, the glitter above her eyes being the most suicidal, leaping like lemmings onto her nose and cheeks.

Is there a moral to my story? Probably not. Buff or thin, I think any compliment is a compliment, even if it isn't the one you expect. Also, matchmaking is a waste of time. You can't make everyone happy all the time or perhaps ever, and you can't pair people up like so many salt and pepper shakers. It just annoys them eventually. You might as well be selfish and just concentration on getting action for yourself.

Oh and if you want someone to remember you drunk out at a bar, spell out your name. For some reason, that does make you more memorable. And having sparkling eyes and a sweet smile doesn't hurt, either.

Happy Birthday, Josh

Friday, August 17th. Josh is a classic New York City story: Beautiful man, perfect body, occasional Broadway dancer. Met him six years ago when he was a bartender at a new bar called REMOTE and I was trying my hand at club promotion. Luke from the bar brought me in to start a hot Tuesday night, two blocks away from Beige at Bowery Bar. Beige had been the hot Tuesday night for years and it was time for its moment to be over. Then on the launch night of my new Tuesday night, Britney and Justin showed up at Beige and, well let's just say it is still the hot Tuesday night party in Manhattan. September 11th helped seal the deal, compelling people to stick with what was old and comfortable in our changing times (*Golden Girls* reruns, M4M chat rooms, Beige) and my club promotion days ended just as quickly as they began. But my friendship with Josh lingered on.

Tonight, Josh invited me to his friend David's apartment for an intimate birthday party. In the intervening years, Josh and I have kept each other on our respective party lists and if I don't run into him infrequently running around town (read: in a gay bar), then this is our best chance to see each other. Of course I wanted to see Josh again, but it is worth mentioning that David has one of the most unique and sensational views from his apartment: straight up Park

Avenue from Union Square with Grand Central Station glittering in the distance. It's always worth a look. And it reminds me of all things fabulous in Manhattan.

I was last in David's apartment in April, following a random night out at Shag with Matty. That night, even Prince Charming made it to David's (although things didn't turn out as Happily Ever After as one might expect). Clay was in town from Texas that time and I joined him and Matty at David's place after the party was already in full swing. David is well known to have the most hot men per square inch of any party on the island, and when I say by the square inch, I mean they are packed in tighter than sardines.

While squeezed in geometrically in the kitchen like walking Tetris pieces, Clay met a ridiculously handsome man who looked just like Prince Charming. In fact, he had played Prince Charming at Walt Disney World before moving to New York, sans white horse. Clay and Prince Charming got on like a house afire and I thought it might truly be a happily ever after. Unfortunately, after a few hot weeks, it burned out just as quickly. Sandra Bullock warned us in *Speed* that relationships developed during situations of intense pressure rarely work out, although I don't think she meant the vacuum-sealed crowd at a gay party.

I fully expected to see Matty back there again and didn't even bother sending him a TXT. I like to surprise Matt by appearing once each decade in just the right place at just the right time. No such luck. However, I did run into Luke also from REMOTE (he had been the manager), now six years later. He hadn't changed much. In fact, he might have still been holding the same cocktail glass in his hand all these years later. I don't know that I have ever seen him without one. Josh was the only person I thought I would know at the party, so it was nice to run into someone else with a familiar face. I had invited Mike ("You know how I love a party... so no."), Ben Harvey ("I am at the MOMA being cultural. But maybe?"), and even, in a moment of desperation not to be alone with strangers, D-A-N from Tuesday night ("Cool. David emailed me earlier. I'll try to make it!"), but alas, I ended up at the party alone with just Josh and Luke to keep me company.

This of course is my least favorite scenario. There is a reason I tried to invite a bunch of people and it isn't just because I am a heartless party guest who doesn't care what fire codes are broken in David's apartment (all of them, by the way). I just hate meeting new people. It is one thing if I am surrounded by friends and I am meeting someone new for third party reasons, like trying to hook up D-A-N with Conor or Ben Harvey. But I absolutely can't stand meeting new people in a place where there are only new people to meet. I don't know what to say, or where to put my hands. And I make that awful sideways crooked smile of mine that just telegraphs my misery at having left the house in the first place.

Everyone was very nice although I managed to put my foot in it again. This is part of the reason why I hate talking to strangers. Okay, it is the whole reason. In my feeble attempts at small talk, I invariably say something that offends the person I am talking to for an unforeseen and therefore unknowable reason. For instance, back in the 90s going home with a guy who was wearing a baseball cap and then making a joke in the car about William Shatner's toupee and then him turning to me and saying, "You haven't seen under this hat yet." The universe got me back for that one less than an hour later when baldy freaked me out by sucking on my toes. That is the story of my life.

So, there was a guy at the party who looked kind of familiar but then again, all gay men seem kind of familiar on a certain level after you live in a city for six or seven years. Not to mention that all gay guys, desperate to fit in and feel accepted in a fantasy high school setting they never seem to graduate from, just generally look alike. Luke's friend was musing out loud that even though the party said that it started at 9:30pm people didn't really show up until eleven.

"Broadway people," I offered, trying to be helpful. "They don't get off until 10:15, 10:30, so they can't get to a party before 11:00pm."

The guy made a bemused grin and asked if I thought the newest arrivals were Broadway people. I pointed to a handsome man in a tight button down shirt over a tight body with a tight 30-something face. "He looks like Broadway people. That's what they look like."

That amused him and later I realized as the conversation progressed that he was himself an actor (hence his familiarity) and probably a Broadway guy too, although I made no effort to lump him in that category when given the chance. How dare I not recognize him from the touring company of who gives a shit! He got me back later though by offering that I might have a future in modeling: for J.C. Penney. Perhaps with a briefcase by a hedge or sweeping small children into a minivan with one hand stiffly tucked into my casual polyester slacks. He looked me dead in the eye as he exacted his revenge from earlier. "There are, you know, the models who are hot, and then there is a whole other category of models who are... well, attractive but not threatening." Point taken.

I suppose I didn't have much reason to be offended, if I even was. After all, he did suggest I could be a model. What's so bad about that? And now that my life is more J.C. Penney than ever, I had to leave at the stroke of 11:45pm to make the 12:10am train home. Suburbia calls, and that call is long distance.

Saw Corey Johnson on my way out. Earlier, Luke had said I hadn't changed and of course he meant in the face where it counts, but I think I have changed in the last six years. And not just in the face. Of course no one has changed more than Corey, sashaying from high school football star to "Miss Thang" with all of the ease and grace of water overflowing from a stopped toilet.

Apparently REMOTE isn't what it used to be either.

"Don't go there again," Josh cautioned," You'll get shot now."

The Paramus TJ Maxx crowd that followed us was one thing, but I don't need any holes in my wool/poly blend blazer. Life in Manhattan is fabulous but it isn't worth dying for. And that minivan isn't going to drive itself.

Starry, Starry Night

Tuesday, August 28th. I didn't want to go to Bowery Bar tonight, but when the stars align, there is little you can do to stem the gravitational pull. Perhaps it was the weird lunar eclipse. After all, my life has been very strange for several days. Maybe I shouldn't look up to the sky for simple answers here on earth.

D-A-N sent me a text message tonight during the show. "Hey. Going to Beige tonight?" No in fact, I planned a rather boring night of heading home and going to bed at a reasonable hour and waking up insanely early (read: 9:00am) to have breakfast with my Dad, who is visiting from Utah and staying in my house. I am already living my life a day late after my car unexpectedly broke down in Virginia on Sunday and I didn't get home until a full 24 hours after I had expected to be there. Now I feel like I am stuck in an alternate universe where Monday is really Tuesday and nothing I had wanted to get done is actually done.

It had been a weird few days. Over the weekend, I had gone to Fredericksburg, Virginia, the town I was born in. We never lived there. My mom hated Fredericksburg, but that was where the hospital was. It is a very quaint city, most notable for George Washington's mother Mary living out her final days there. A few years later, I was born in the hospital named after her and for the past few years, I have emceed their burgeoning gay pride celebration.

I feared coming back for a third time might be a mistake and it was. The new pride board (always an early warning sign of trouble ahead) was headed up by a lesbian who decided to turn the event into a tribute to her girlfriend. At one point, her girlfriend was spontaneously led up on stage and handed a bouquet of flowers while the head of pride did a ceremonial dance in front of the stage in her honor. Meanwhile, I patiently organized the snack tables in the volunteer area in a shady, bug-riddled corner wondering why I had driven six hours to sit in the hot shade when I could have just stayed home with air conditioning and my own bed.

The real reason I had gone down there was to further a romance I had started the previous year with a cute local guy named Ryan, who lived in Fredericksburg but was born in Kentucky. Ryan has a lovely accent which combined with my radio deafness makes him virtually impossible to understand. According to my roommate Mike, it is something of a two-way street since Ryan never seems to understand what I am saying and most of the time we just carry on two completely independent conversations but in a back and forth fashion that makes it seem to the casual observer like we were talking to each other. Fortunately, conversation wasn't on the top of our list of things to do. Well, it wasn't on my list.

For some reason, Ryan was not in a frisky mood. It probably had to do with the fact that he started dating someone between the time he invited me to come down and stay with him during pride weekend and the time I actually arrived. This is a common long distance gay phenomenon. And instead of having me stay in a hotel or tell me this was happening, he just turned frigid and pretended nothing was wrong, while avoiding his new boyfriend on the street when I was around. The whole thing left me very annoyed and impatient and we had the kind of fight where I am furious and he doesn't say anything and I storm out of town in a huff, but not before buying an ice cream cone and swinging through an antique store and stuffing a small writing desk in the backseat of my convertible.

Maybe ten miles out of town, the lights start flashing on my dash and the car begins to violently overheat. It was a very warm and humid day but this was worse than you would expect, even for my ancient clunker. I pulled over to the side of the road and bought coolant at a nearby gas station. That didn't seem to satisfy the problem so eventually I got towed to the nearest thing that passed for a town and was told that no one could work on my car until morning. Refusing to call Ryan for help after the horrible scene I had made in his attic apartment, I spent the night in a 1950s Colonial version of the Bates Motel eating snacks from the gas station and dinner at a local Burger King that was within walking distance, paralyzed with twin fears of either being murdered in my room or what was growing in the shower, the sink drain and on the bedspread.

The next day I drove from the tire center to which I had been towed to a small specialty mechanic less than a mile away, tucked quietly in the back of an office park in the middle of nowhere. The owner/mechanic was a hot stud who looked like porn star Ken Ryker, admittedly a personal favorite and he had two little latino twinks running around doing his bidding. I felt like I was in a gay version of Punk'd directed by Chi Chi La Rue. The mechanic had a sweet loyal dog that followed him around and I spent my morning tossing a tennis ball for him and hoping the mechanic would fall in love with me, insist that I quit my job in New York City and move with him to rural Virginia. As you can see, in times of quiet and boredom, my mind makes up a wide variety of insane notions.

For some reason, the whole car had overheated to the point that all of the belts in it had melted and snapped. So, after all the belts were replaced and it was deemed roadworthy, I bade a sad, longing farewell to the hunky mechanic who to my disappointment but not surprise did not kiss me good-bye and I continued on my way to New York. It was too late for me to make the show that night so I just ended up driving home and preparing the house for my Dad who was coming to stay with me the next day. Oh yes and pack for my trip to New Orleans on Friday.

So with all that going on, I decided to leave my bar going decision up to fate and asked celebrity party planner and the show's guest host for the evening: Wade Williams.

"Are we going to Bowery Bar tonight?"

"Yes! How did you know?"

So after the show ended, Wade and I decamped to his hotel a few blocks away to drop off his bag and gaze at the lobby swimming pool with the swim up bar. All straight people frolicking in the water but at least there was one guy who was reasonably attractive in his bathing suit. You really can't ask for more in life. From the hotel, we journeyed down to B-Bar with the chattiest cab driver this side of Taxi Cab Confessions. He lives up near Columbia (111th and Broadway) while his girlfriend lives next to B-Bar (Bowery and 4th). Apparently, he was fresh out of the Army where he spent the last 20 years creating tactical scenarios for the NSA. Good thing our nation doesn't depend on his discretion any longer since he leaks like a colander.

When we arrived I sent a text message to D-A-N to find out where he was, you know, since going was his idea in the first place. I wasn't really sure what was happening with him, or I should say us. I had only started talking to him because I was trying to fix him up with one or more of my friends, but since I gave him my number at Bowery Bar two weeks earlier, we had been texting back and forth a bit. It was nothing really flirtatious or anything, but a little more intense than new casual acquaintances. Maybe there was nothing to it and I was just being hopeful because his arms were so big in his tight t-shirts and unlike most hot guys, he didn't seem to take an instant dislike to me.

Turns out D-A-N was at Pieces for karaoke with his friends, so Wade and I settled at a table with drinks in hand. So much for that rendezvous. In the meantime, Ari Gold was at the next table, ready to gently chide me about our "diva" dust-up on the air two weeks ago.

In talking about my various pride adventures on air, I might have mentioned that I thought Ari had been a "diva" earlier this year at Pride South Florida. Maybe it was because I was kept waiting at the hotel for an hour and a half, unable to actually emcee the show because he wouldn't release the town car we were sharing while he did his sound check. Or perhaps it was because he asked to see me before he went on stage to find out how I was going to introduce him since he "wanted to make sure I knew who he was" even though I had already introduced him a half dozen times at other events and we had just had him on as a guest on the radio show three days earlier. Or maybe it was because one of his back-up dancers came up to me backstage and asked me if he was always such a diva.

Naturally, our listeners being the snitchy bitches that they are, they couldn't wait to run to Ari's website to email him about how we had been slamming him on air. And the next night during the show, his manager Rich started IMing me saying that Ari wanted to come on the show and playfully defend himself.

"It will be fun!" he insisted but I knew it would be a disaster and tried to warn him away. Ari, like most celebrities or in his case those who believe they are celebrities, has no sense of humor about himself. And even if he tried to be cute about it, I knew he would come off as defensive (he did) and just make it worse for himself (he did) by showing everyone that he was, not just a diva, but even worse than I had let on. "See. I am not so diva-like that I wouldn't come over to say hello," he purred days later at Bowery Bar trying to show that trademark sense of humor he lacks. After all, it was I who walked over to him.

Charlie wandered in, still carrying that same old book. Charlie is a recent law school grad who is enjoying reading for pleasure again, although he is making extremely slow work of his current tome. As I do with any lawyer, I cornered him with my panoramic misunderstanding of the law and tried to engage him with my latest wild opinion. I attempted to impress him with my dim theory about the connection between gay marriage and kosher food. A recent unpopular (with Jews) appeals court ruling allowed the government to set a less strict standard for what can be sold and marketed as kosher since, while originally a religious standard, it now has a broader understanding in the marketplace and therefore did not need to be tied to the most conservative interpretation of the word. Alas, he was more interested in my church-state discussion about Christmas trees at City Halls. And here I thought I could just be boring at home.

Ben Harvey finally arrived just in time for Charlie to beat a hasty exit. "I am just not feeling it tonight" he had told me as he collapsed into the wrought iron patio chair less than thirty minutes earlier. I don't think my legal wrangling after a long day of legal wrangling improved conditions either. True to his word, Travels With Charlie closed another chapter, even before Ben could wend his way through the tightly packed crowd.

Ben was as cute as ever, with his Harvard friend Ryan in tow. Ever since that editor tortured me during my one year syndication deal, I am wary of gays with Ivy League educations. Then again, that editor is supposedly straight now, last I heard, although I suspect no less annoying to those of us who use the English language like a fly swatter. Harvard Ryan seemed nice, but as usual, I was more interested in Ben than in his friends. Ben caught the eye of a cutie in a red polo shirt, and I even forcefully prodded him to make the first move. Although I don't think anything came of it. My natural curiosity led me to discover on Friendster.com that he was a musician named Greg, which I think is more information than Ben got that night.

Just as I was ready to leave, everything kicked into high gear. After no word from D-A-N in two hours, I sent him a "heading home" text message that revealed a quick response that he was, in fact, now at the bar. Much searching found gay nightlife fixture Corey Johnson casually orbiting one sexy hunk after another, although D-A-N was more difficult to spot. To be fair, I had only seen him that one time before and despite perfect vision, gay bars are too filled with music, lights and pretty for me to effectively search for anything or anyone amidst the sensory overload.

I finally found him on the dance floor with a cluster of friends. Still cute, with a winning smile, Clark Kent hair and solid arms. Polite chat about karaoke (he sang a song from Les Miserables) and houseguests staying too long (four day weekend fine, anything longer too long), but nothing worth sacrificing sleep or writing in great detail about. Maybe I was just dazzled by his arms and sweet smile and there was nothing more between us. Moments later, he was gone.

The real excitement came after he left when Wade introduced me to a not-out actor on a hit TV show recently signed to star in a hit movie franchise reboot. I wonder if Michael Musto, who was there, saw him too. I tried to play it cool by not talking about his TV show and then later realized that I should have mentioned that we had the creator of his show on our radio show. Wade insisted he would want to be a guest on our show, but I wouldn't hold my openly gay breath on that one.

Then Ben Harvey was found standing with actors Peter Stickles and Michael Carbanaro. Michael is too adorable for words and like all magicians; he knows keenly where his hands are at all times. Unfortunately, I will have to experience his particular brand of magic on another day. As always, the drunk train beckons and I can't miss my last ride home for the night. I am already a day behind schedule as it is!

Next time it will be one-on-one with Ben. Just the two of us in the quiet corner of a bar with no Charlie to observe or simple names of hunky accountants to spell. No houses to clean or Dads visiting. I caught Michael's eye and waved a final good bye as Wade and I headed for a taxi. The driver was quiet this time, which was just what the doctor ordered after such a busy environment and a hectic few days. No national security secrets to divulge. Just a seamless ride up Third Avenue in the middle of the night. Perfect.

See. Sometimes, even if it is just for a moment, the stars do line up.

Heal, Conor, Heal

Friday, August 31st. I relish my anonymity, such as it is. Of course I have a radio show, which has an audience. But the audience is far away from where I live. So it's easy to forget, if the phone doesn't ring during the show or after work at a bar, that I have even the smallest measure of fame. Even when I blog, with entry after entry languishing without public comment, I feel virtually unknown. I get to believe that I exist only in a void, a vacuum, with just the noisy isolated chaos of my own thoughts racing through my head to keep me company. It's nice.

This may seem like a contradictory notion for someone who has so aggressive put themselves out into the public space. It is not like there is the same groundswell of demand for information about me that you see, for instance, when a celebrity is embroiled in a scandal, or when Britney Spears goes to Starbucks for a cup of coffee. I suppose it is my Gemini moon in play and my double Scorpio nature. I crave privacy and attention simultaneously which can be a delicate if precarious balance. Writing and doing radio gives me the best of both worlds. I am heard but rarely seen. And with most of my audience far away from where I live and play, my day-to-day existence can be downright ordinary.

The only times I have ever been recognized in the city were in bars and the first time was at Barracuda some months ago. I returned to the scene of the crime last night with my roommate Mike. Since moving away, we have both fallen off the social radar, Mike even more than me. At least with the radio show, I am constantly interacting with people who are inviting me out or appearing in things that require attending. But ultimately, since we both live far out of town, we exist in the same suburban boat and the only way to maintain a social life under these circumstances is to force ourselves to make the time. And with fall TV looming in a couple of weeks, better to get into the swing of things now while there is still time.

Building my friendship with Ben Harvey is a twin mission of mine, so we headed to the bar to meet up with him. We have a lovely friendship that is more about the fame of other people than our own. Our recent shared obsession with Rosie on *The View* was just the tip of the pop culture iceberg. However, Ben gets concerned sometimes that if one of our evenings hanging out together isn't interesting enough, I will fail to blog about it, committing our banal existences to the obscurity they truly deserve. This is an unnecessary worry. As I assured him with my last blog posting, there is no sow's ear so paper thin that I couldn't stitch a silk purse out of it.

My memory is terrible and when much of what you want to remember is a drunken, hazy blur, the odds are it won't last until morning, let alone make a notable appearance in some future biography. This is the real reason that I write my blog. The radio show burns a lot of my creative energy, and doesn't leave me much for the swim back. Since the launch of the show, I have struggled to finish not just writing books but reading them. So blogging about every minor trip out of the house keeps the old tools sharp, or at least that is what I tell myself.

The best part of my blog of course is the detective work I use to track down the random strangers that I spy out and about. For this Friendster.com is a stalker's dream. Two or three random bits of information, a few key strokes and in no time, detailed personal information is available to any of the nearly dozen people who visit my blog. Ben enjoys this aspect of the blog and he isn't the only one. I estimate about ten people read my blog and virtually all of them visit to see if they are back in it again when it updates semi-annually.

It wasn't my intention to go out, just like Tuesday night. But Ben had emailed me days ago, and I missed it until early yesterday morning (or hours too late depending on your perspective). I read my mail obsessively, rarely going more than an hour between full sweeps of all of my contact points. My personal email and my office email are checked obsessively all day. Even MySpace is never left for more than a few minutes during waking hours.

But I recently created a secret email address with the intention that very close friends and family members would be able to reach me when my more public email addresses became so overwhelmed with fan mail that the real mail I wanted would get lost. This of course has not happened because I am apparently neither famous nor interesting enough to warrant more than a message or two here and there. And combined with my constant attention to my various online mail points, the whole thing is so beyond manageable it is downright uninteresting.

So, I have a private email but I forget to read it all the time. No one writes me there. So it is just too depressing to visit day after day to see that nothing has changed. Sometimes I get spam, but even that might not happen for days at a time. Really only Ben and Jennifer, host of *Whatever with Alexis and Jennifer* over on the Martha Channel actively email me there, and Jennifer is on vacation this week so I have been especially lax.

But Ben had emailed me after midnight last night saying that he was going out to Barracuda TOMORROW (his emphasis in all caps) and I remembered him commenting on my funny insistence on carefully using the word tomorrow in my emails because I usually write them at 3am, making the word ambiguous to most earnest observers or those who also are awake and checking email in the middle of the night (like Ben).

So I sent him a text message during the show just to make sure that he meant Friday and not Thursday and of course

TOMORROW was tonight, and always anxious to see him again, I agreed to dash off for a quick drink before heading home to pack, make breakfast for my visiting Dad and fly off to New Orleans for a long weekend of booze, beignets and boys at Southern Decadence.

At Barracuda, Ben arrived again with his friend Harvard Ryan in tow, along with assorted actorly characters. His visiting friend Dave, the "Al Roker of Australia" who is in fact, hot and thin. Eric Michael, an actual actor, who is loathe to say he is an actor for fear of people thinking he is primarily a waiter.

"Working actor" I told him, "That's what you need to say." This is especially if you don't want to be confused with the homeless.

As usual, I could only get two new names so the actor from HERE TV's vampire opus *The Lair* and the guy who looks like my hot bartender friend Josh but with even more intense eyebrows will have to go nameless. There might have even been another guy floating around there too, but there was just too much gay in our circle to keep an easy focus.

I wasn't the only one having trouble. It was too many people for Ben to juggle at once, and it felt a little like he was trying to manage a party in his own apartment. It is easier to host the Malaria virus than to try to host a gathering inside a gay bar. Too many working parts. And Peter Stickles swirling around in the air like Tinkerbell the whole time, flashing and flinging pixie dust, and my roommate camouflaged in the corner to blend in with the wall did not help Ben in his herding efforts at all.

And I have always loved Barracuda, but it is a small neighborhood bar that tends to get very crowded. This is not the kind of place to try to have a drink with eight of your closest friends and then expect to actually have a conversation with any of them. The back space in the bar is more of a lounge but sometimes there is a drag queen screeching in the narrow strip of a stage which makes talking impossible. Even when there isn't a show going on, the pool table with a worn out plank of plywood over it makes for an awkward centerpiece near the DJ booth.

The front bar has some café tables which are always filled with dirty cocktail glasses; a long bench along a mirrored wall is the final resting spot of the mildly cruisy. When it is packed, you can often find yourself uncomfortably riding up on top of the ancient pinball machine in moments that can remind one not so tastefully of a certain scene from *The Accused*. Ben and company stationed themselves in the center of the front bar and did their level best to maintain a perimeter in a drunken brawl filled with interloping encroachers.

After a while, the density of a crowd starts to get to me and makes me as edgy as a second pot of coffee in the morning. Then suddenly Conor appeared, his intense yet oddly reassuring gaze as soothing as that of a border collie. Conor makes me laugh which doesn't happen very often for me, making it all the harder to cut the evening short to catch the 12:10am train to suburbia.

I like funny people because, despite all outward appearances, I don't like being the center of attention. If you don't believe me, you are in good company because neither do any of my friends. But it is true that I am always drawn to people who are more famous, more loud, better grammarians or prettier than I am so that I can enjoy being in the audience.

I like being in the hurricane of attention, but in the less troublesome outer bands, orbiting around a strong, organized eye. It is more fun for me to not have to work all the time, and being with the crowd, instead of in front of it, is my natural state of being.

To Live And Dine In LA

Wednesday, September 5th. I almost died yesterday in New Orleans.

To be fair, it is New Orleans. If you don't almost die when you are visiting, you aren't doing it right. I started going to New Orleans every year for Southern Decadence after the city was hit by the double whammy of Hurricane Katrina and blowhard Jerry Falwell blaming the hurricane on the gays. I figured that if there is anything gays do well, it is travel all the time and spend piles of disposable income. Like many cities, New Orleans has an economy that relies heavily on tourists. It seemed to me, that the best thing we could do as a community to both give Falwell the finger and bring the city back was to visit and spend money.

So every year, I come during the Labor Day weekend celebration of Southern Decadence. Billed as gay Mardi Gras, the festivities are tamer now than they had been in years past. The birth of the internet woke the larger world up to the sweaty sea of public sex that was a bridge too far for local politicians used to turning a blind eye to a wide array of depraved consensual acts. Okay, so it isn't as decadent as it used to be, and you can't get a blow job on the street the way some people order a hot dog from a vending cart in

Manhattan but it is still a whole lot of fun. And I personally prove that you don't need to be lewd in order to be dangerous.

In my vain pursuit of the kind of eternal life promised in the iconic *Death Becomes Her*, I participate in an anti-aging program in New York. This is exactly the kind of fruity liberal elite activity Fox News loves to rail against as presented by an array of news babes no doubt featuring *Logan's Run*-style expiration dates themselves. Love the new face, Greta! In my own defense, I discovered the program while watching TV which says as much about my susceptibility to anything pitched on television as it does about my youth obsession, which is admittedly unhealthy on both counts.

The program requires me to inject myself with hormones and to take a fistful of vitamins and other supplements twice each day. I used to take my anti-aging vitamins two at a time, an insanely slow process that, like jogging, probably wipes out any advance I might get in years by sucking up that extra time in the very activity that is designed to create time in the first place.

One day, my Grandmother frustrated by my glacial pill-popping pace snapped, "Oh for crying out loud, open your throat and swallow them all at once." So for the last year and a half, not wanting to seem like a pussy in front of her, that is how I have done it. A fistful of pills thrown down my throat, which had been a fine system until yesterday when life once again imitated the art of *30 Rock* and the vitamins got lodged in my throat.

Suddenly the image of Liz Lemon giving herself the Heimlich against a chair and Jack's casual observation that "I would think that choking alone in your apartment would be your number one fear" were flashing through my brain as I struggled to breathe.

Moments later, I was coughing and puking in the sink until three of them came back up. That was enough clearing for me to swallow some large swigs of water to get the rest of them down. But standing there alone in my underwear in the hotel room, my face red and puffy from the hacking, just served to remind me of the running theme of the weekend: we are just too old for this.

Never mind that it was anti-aging vitamins I was choking on, the whole weekend was an endurance test for the liver, kidneys, stomach and feet. Each day began at the crack of one, with a sumptuous lunch that left my friends and me incapacitated and in need of a nap. We'd regroup at 8pm for another massive meal and then head to the Bourbon Pub for a night of intense intoxication.

For three days, I battled nausea from overeating, overdrinking, and rapid changes in temperature moving from air conditioned interiors to searing humid exteriors. The combination of sweltering heat and a basket of fried pickles I refused to abandon even when beyond stuffed nearly caused my complete and utter gastric demise on a street corner on Sunday afternoon. What can I say? I have no will power. And New Orleans is not the place to visit if you lack impulse control.

Out at the bars, everyone was too old for their outfit, me included. I understand the gay desire to never get any older because I am both team captain and star player, but I just don't know if an ANF muscle tee, cargo shorts and a sideways baseball cap are appropriate attire on a charter member of AARP. To paraphrase Helen Gurley Brown, I will wear shorts until I die, but that doesn't mean it will be pretty. I suppose the most important thing is that everyone was having fun, and when you are on the shady side of fifty, really how many more days of fun are left?

I spent a lot of time this weekend in the VIP room at the Bourbon Pub, thanks in large part to my friendship with Chi Chi La Rue. Chi Chi is well known around the globe as arguably the world's most famous porn director, which might have something to do with the fact that he is also a larger than life character notable for appearing in public in drag.

Most of the time, I see her when we are drunk and he is in drag so the use and misuse of pronouns is generally as blurry as my memories. Over the years, Chi Chi and I have developed a lovely friendship and he has Sirius Radio in his car and is not afraid to call into the show. Chi Chi is my favorite kind of celebrity: one who helps reinforce the delusion that I am famous too.

Listeners of my radio show and my disgruntled roommate may think I am famous, but I am largely unknown even in the gay community. Trust me. I shamelessly push myself at every turn. I just don't think there is the kind of public clamor for me that would keep the ball rolling all the way to superstardom. To be fair however, my privacy is still very important to me, so my lack of success making a name for myself is a situation I continue to relish even as it keeps me standing in lines and denied access to free cocktails. So this means any appearance in a VIP room ends up being thanks to the largesse of a genuine celebrity like Chi Chi.

My anonymity is worth the trade off. What can I say? Walking unmolested down a supermarket aisle is more important to me than sashaying on a red carpet, although in a dream world I would be able to do both. To be fair to the Bourbon Pub, the bar manager knows me but his staff doesn't. And instead of making one of those dreadful "don't you know who I think I am" scenes, I just opted to ride in on the La Rue train.

Friday night Chi Chi La Rue was holding court on the third floor of the Bourbon Pub, the kind of ancient attic annex Anne Frank would have felt right at home in. Chi Chi was there with notorious drag sensation Lady Bunny who had just finished her set and made her way, drink firmly in hand, to a stool in the center of the room, if not also the center of the attention. Chi Chi had been DJing all afternoon long and was clearly ready for a drink or five by the time I arrived upstairs.

Lady Bunny was perched in the middle of everything, quiet save for the occasional dramatic outburst. Bunny was acting in her own movie, primarily *Valley of the Dolls* although she did slip in and out of Bette Davis when the occasion called for it.

Chi Chi's hot phrase of the evening was "I'd love to do it, but I can't brisket." He would usually cap the new catchphrase with dramatic effect by staring you in the eye while clamping his rouged lips down on the straw in his drink and taking a quick sip. My love of a good pun knows no bounds and the next day at the Old Chartres House, I just had to order the BBQ brisket po-boy sandwich in honor of it.

As the night wore on, Bunny's wig got progressively scarier and scarier. The combination of the late night and the humidity took its toll on that wiry heap of plastic yarn that looked like the Lady had scalped a Barbie beauty head circa 1972. "Tell everything! Include diagrams!" Chi Chi urged in between briskets, but I can't really draw.

Chi Chi demanded that Lady Bunny show me her brown-stained pantyhose, which she insisted was from Bunny shitting herself. Bunny claimed it was a gumbo mishap but two hours later she was still in those same messy hose, still perched precariously on that same damned stool. I am pretty sure the stained hose was from a bit during Lady Bunny's show involving splattering chocolate pudding on her legs and letting the audience think that she shit herself. Or she could have just shit herself. It's Lady Bunny. I wouldn't put anything past her. And I would have gotten up close to make the determination for myself but I couldn't brisket.

The only thing dirtier than Bunny's legs was the carpet. I dubbed it the night of 1000 spilled drinks, although I only managed to spill one of them. In fact, the whole attic was in a woeful state of disrepair. A colony of cats live up there to keep the mice and rats away and that only adds to the crazy lady house of it all. Boxes are stacked up haphazardly and pieces of furniture are arranged around them to approximate a living room environment but it all just looks like *The Odd Couple*'s apartment if Felix died and Oscar never went looking for the body.

At one point, some cutie boys insisted that their friend come up and audition for Chi Chi. This happens quite regularly since I witnessed it myself in Minneapolis during pride in June. Chi Chi was working as a DJ that weekend and a dirty boy started dancing on a box while Chi Chi was spinning. The more Chi Chi looked past him, the harder he started grinding. He was a heaving filthy whore mess by closing time when Chi Chi was so drunk she started yelling for someone, anyone to find the purse in her hands. Honey, if she is so blind drunk she can't see her own purse, she certainly isn't going to see you opening your hole like the Carlsbad Caverns on a box in the middle of the dance floor.

Back at the Bourbon, I reminded Chi Chi of our Minneapolis adventure which prompted a great story while we were waiting about two men getting it on right next to her on a pool table once while she was trying to just sit and enjoy her cocktail. And the more she ignored them, the more aggressive they got, to the point where they were fully engaged with their legs thrown across Chi Chi's lap. I love the image of Chi Chi politely sitting on that pool table, no doubt ankles crossed like a lady as those two went to town right next to her, probably getting more pleasure out of their frustration than she ever would have from looking.

The hunk finally arrived upstairs in the VIP room and he was a handsome thirty-something with a tight body. Chi Chi asked to see his cock. "But I'm not hard," he whined.

"I didn't ask for a story. I asked to see your cock."

He whipped it out and even soft, it was quite big and thick. Chi Chi clutched me like a new car winner on *The Price Is Right*. "Oh my God! Did you see that? It's huge!" It sort of surprised me that Chi Chi, after all these years in porn, could still get excited about seeing a new cock. I guess that is a lesson for us all when we are feeling old. A weekend in New Orleans may play out like a heartburn commercial when you are thirty-something (or older), but that doesn't mean it's too late to enjoy it anyway.

As if the French Quarter wasn't wild enough, my ex-boyfriend Mitch was in town. Now to call him simply my ex is to dismiss the on-going saga of our relationship. Mitch is a difficult situation to explain because it is one of those times in my life where I dated someone and never really broke up with them, but for one reason or another, drifted apart. Sometimes, one of us leaves town. In Mitch's case he took leave of his senses.

So we have had an on and off thing for years. I guess you might call it fuck buddies or friends with benefits but I don't think either of those tired clichés really covers it. I mean, a fuck buddy is someone you hardly know and have no interest in knowing further but you like getting it on. A friend with benefits says to me that it is someone you do like and you know and occasionally you fall into bed together because you know it wouldn't make a good relationship but you are both horny and comfortable so why not.

The moment I met Mitch, no, the moment I saw Mitch, I knew I would know him for the rest of my life. And I didn't think we would be married and living happily ever after either. I just knew he would always be around. And that is exactly how the last ten years or so have gone. He has moved, I have moved. We have both dated other people. But through the years we have kept in contact, sexually and otherwise. He was even my ten year high school reunion date, because who doesn't want to go to their reunion with a hot blond former porn star. Maybe our timing wasn't right, or perhaps it was just never meant to be. But being around each other is so comfortable because we understand each other and as I get older, I realize how important it is to have that in another person, even if you aren't a couple.

Now Mitch is a free spirit, much wilder than I am. He has an intense sexual magnetism that draws random gay guys to him like instant deranged stalkers. Going to New Orleans for Southern Decadence for someone like Mitch is like hot gluing a hungry fat kid to a conveyor belt in a candy factory. So while I had hoped to spend some time with him on the trip (after all, he was with me when I almost exploded on the sidewalk from all the booze and fried pickles at lunch), I figured that sex was probably out of the question. He likes me and all but we've done it before, and the city was filled to the dirty cat-filled rafters with new men.

So when Mitch texted me at 2am to find out where I was and I invited him to join me up in the attic VIP room at the Bourbon Pub with Lady Bunny and Chi Chi La Rue, I knew he would be in his debauched element and I wouldn't stick around much longer. I knew I was delivering the lion to the meat den and wasn't interested in seeing the carnage.

Before Mitch got upstairs, Lady Bunny crawled away from her stool, although come to think of it, she may have crawled away with the stool. All I know is, one minute she was there on the stool and the next minute, she and the stool had vanished like in a magic act. This is what having six or ten drinks will do to you. Time starts skipping and it is hard to keep track of the players anymore.

Mitch and Chi Chi had known each other years earlier when Mitch was a young porn pup in West Hollywood but like almost everyone he had known in his former life in Los Angeles, they had long since lost contact. I don't know if Chi Chi actually remembered him, but she liked him again right away because Mitch has the kind of easy-going confidence you often find in men with big hearty cocks who know they have big hearty cocks. They have nothing to prove.

That hot guy from earlier with the big cock had left which was fine because he, for whatever reason, did not share Mitch's swagger. But this being New Orleans and Southern Decadence, he was soon replaced by other hot guys and other cocks and things in the dirty attic took a decidedly sexual turn.

The next thing I knew Mitch was in the midst of it all and that was my cue to leave. For years he lived a life without conventional rules except when he was around me, which at the time contributed to him not spending much time with me. After all, why have any impulse control at all if no one around you expects or often even wants it? But the years had changed him and he takes more control of himself now even as the rest of the world still longs to pull his pants off.

I could tell he was hesitant at first because I was there. It is hard to want to be good and bad at the same time and I didn't want to get in the way of the fun. I don't mind being the angel on his shoulder but not here, not now. Mitch saw me leave but he knew even without looking that I wouldn't want to stick around for all that was to come next. As I walked down the stairs back into the now half-empty club, I took the final vestiges of civilization with me and the animals raged until dawn on a worn-out leather sofa that would never be the same again.

It didn't bother me. That was Mitch in his element and definitely me out of mine. Orgies are just not my thing. Even if he hadn't been there, I would have left anyway. Though it was strange to see someone sucking his cock, it was amusing because Chi Chi was sitting right next to the guy directing the scene. Mitch was happy. Chi Chi was happy. And in my own way, I was happy too. New Orleans can often be a place without limits and, in a way, you have to create your own boundaries, lest you be swept away in the swelling tide of hedonism.

For me, the French Quarter is about the food and the alcohol, a gastronomic orgy of unfathomable depravity. I literally will eat until I am beyond sick and then have a little more. I relish my long afternoon naps alone when I am stuffed from lunch and lolling around while the heat and humidity rage somewhere else outside. I hideaway in my hidden gem of a cheap hotel, off the beaten path where I can rest in peace. For others, the sexual exploration is the reason to come back year after year. But for me, the real joy is somewhere else.

I hope this anti-aging program keeps me going, not so I can be forever young, but so that I will be alive for more trips down to the Big Easy for that delicious shrimp and tomato in tasso cream sauce at The Gumbo Shop and the fried pickles at the Praline Connection. Just a few extra mornings of coffee and beignets at Café du Monde and that heart-clogging burger and stuffed baked potato at Port of Call that caps every trip. I live to eat, and if I am going to die choking, I hope it's on that.

The Life Of Riley

Monday, September 10th. I have a lot of empathy for my friend Chi Chi La Rue and frankly all of my friends who toil in the porn industry. It is a life that so many envy but at the end of the day it is a job like any other, even if it does come with the perk of copious amounts of hot naked people. I promise you that it is often more trouble than it is worth.

As I had been a couple of days ago, last year I was also in New Orleans for Southern Decadence, hanging out with adorable porn star Roman Heart. Roman's beautiful voice is the same perfect blend of sweet and hard as his famous face, and his tight body is completely without flaw. We didn't have much time to hang out since he was working constantly and spent most of the weekend in various tiny briefs, gingerly stepping over glasses and spilled drinks in between half-hearted dance moves on top of the downstairs bar at the Bourbon Pub.

It is dangerous work made only more delightful by the constant attempts by the patrons to give the dancers colonoscopies with wadded up dollar bills. It's funny. Only in the world of stripping do women routinely make vastly more money than their male counterparts. A woman will barely look at you in a strip club for less than a twenty but gay men expect a lot for a lowly single.

After a while, I had wandered upstairs to the VIP room and ran into Chi Chi. It was moments before she was to go on stage and lovingly berate the "filthy" crowd as she does. But just then, as the DJ was bringing down the music for her to leap on stage, she realized something was missing and started screaming for her cardboard box. Suddenly, there it was, racing toward her in the hands of some insanely skinny gay boy in bikini bottoms and sneakers. A non-descript cardboard box labeled "For Chi Chi Only! Touch It And Die!"

Even without opening it, I knew exactly what it was. This was the box of giveaway porn, the stock and trade of gay bar stage performances. When Romaine and I travel for the show, we also have "the box" and while it is sometimes filled with porn, it is more likely to be stuffed with t-shirts or mardi gras beads. The crowd doesn't love you unless you give them something free and they love nothing more than free porn. It was in that moment at the Bourbon Pub that I realized how similar my life on the road was to Chi Chi's and how grateful I was that I didn't have to do it in a dress, wig and heels.

Chi Chi loves the unknown of the moment. She is spontaneous and loves to surprise and be surprised. I am certain it is this desire to keep things interesting and unpredictable that is the key to her longevity in an industry that could, for obvious reasons, become very routine, very quickly.

While on stage at the Bourbon Pub last year, female porn star Savannah Samson, who beat me in a tie for a Gay VN Award earlier this year for Best Non-Sex Performance in a porn film, descended from the ceiling during Chi Chi's show to huge cheers from the crowd. Seizing the moment in typical fashion, Chi Chi popped Savannah's stocking foot in her mouth. The crowd went crazy, not knowing in that moment that after walking across the cat infested rafters of the Bourbon Pub, her foot was covered in hair. Chi Chi came off stage and greeted me spitting the cat hair out. "I'm still waiting for the hairball to come up," she confided good-naturedly.

I always see Chi Chi when she is working. Not directing films, but the rest of the world that goes along with being a famous personality. It is a job that never ends as long as there is a third person in the room. Chi Chi spends a lot of time DJing now, which is a personal passion that adds a nice dimension to the promotional travel she does anyway. She has such joie d vivre and it is infectious. People are drawn to Chi Chi. They want to talk to her, get her attention, but most importantly, they live to please her.

Chi Chi has that powerful personal effect on people. For years now we have welcomed porn stars, men and women, gay and straight, onto our show who have done scenes that Chi Chi directed.

They all told the same story. They were very clear walking in what they wanted to do and what they didn't want to do. But somehow in the midst of the scene, Chi Chi changed their minds and they found themselves enthusiastically doing things they had never dreamed of. I have wondered for quite some time now just what it is about Chi Chi that creates situations like that.

I think it might be her utter exuberance about everything. She is just so excited, and when someone is cheering you on so vigorously, it is hard to say no. And I am sure it helps that she isn't afraid to get her own hands dirty in the process, as evidenced by the mouth full of cat hair.

It reminded me of a story JoBeth Williams told about being in the pool near the end of *Poltergeist*. With all the lights and equipment around, it was very dangerous and she could have been electrocuted at any moment. But Steven Spielberg stood in the water with her the whole time so that if she fried, he would fry too, and there wasn't anyone on the set who wanted to be responsible for killing the most commercially successful director/producer of the day.

I suppose it is a combination of this aspect of her personality and my empathy for her that turns me into Chi Chi's personal assistant whenever I see her lately. And it's not Chi Chi demanding that I wait on her hand and foot. But there is just something about her that makes me happy to get her a fresh cocktail or carry her suitcase full of CDs around.

In June, I was in Minneapolis for Twin Cities Pride and, being a native Minnesotan, Chi Chi was in town as well working as a DJ at a local club in between visiting family. Chi Chi was thrilled I was in town and invited me to join her and some of the porn boys as they got ready at the hotel before heading to the club.

As usual, I was in shorts and a t-shirt. When I arrived, Chi Chi was already dressed to the nines and just pulling together last final things. It was the porn boys, swirling in and out of the room half naked, debating tank tops and inspecting muscle definition in the mirror that sucked up all the time. But Chi Chi was calm in the middle of this hurricane for her attention.

Out at the club everyone wanted some attention. The porn boys Chi Chi brought with her for the weekend, the various patrons, even the club manager. Through it all, she sipped gently on a long series of cocktails, danced in place to keep the party going and when the porn boys would devolve into pre-teen girls, shoot me a knowing look and a wink. At the end of the evening, I took charge of Chi Chi's CD case. She was hammered drunk and would occasionally panic when she couldn't find the purse that was in her left hand.

From the club we all piled into taxis and headed to someone's apartment for an after party. At the apartment were several of the local drag performers and Chi Chi knew them all from way back. I lingered around, making sure that Chi Chi's all important CD case didn't end up lost and flirted hopelessly with some local blond boy who had almost no interest in me after one of Chi Chi models who had less than no interest in me left the party with someone else. Even still, it was a very fun adventure with Chi Chi guarding her CD case and three months later I was back on the job.

Chi Chi is in New York this weekend to DJ at the HustlaBall. Now I had never been before, but it is exactly what it sounds like. It is a big porn star-studded event featuring dozens of performers and escorts mingling and having fun with three packed floors of potential customers. When we arrived the Rentboy.com people who were throwing the party and the HustlaBall staff just assumed I was Chi Chi's assistant, which was fine with me. It is part of what I love about being in New York City. No one here has Sirius Radio and they don't care that I talk for a living. This coming weekend when I go to Dallas, I won't be able to walk down the street without being recognized. It's nice to spend an evening being not just an ordinary person, but even better, an unimportant one, since it is a more accurate reflection of my real life than the kind of attention I get when I travel for work promoting the show. I only wish it hadn't been such a struggle to get a free drink, but I guess that is the trade off of anonymity.

The only people at the event tonight who knew I even had a real job were prior guests on the show. It felt like everyone was there tonight. Barrett Long, who was also in New Orleans last weekend was there with new roommate Jason Crew, whom I first met on the set of *Big Rig* two years ago making my non-sex porn debut. That's a lot of trouble for one household. The third musketeer was the ever delicious Rod Barry. He was upset about something and after some shots started getting belligerent. We danced a bit until his playful punching got too painful and I pawned him off on Barrett Long, who seemed to have more experience with unhappy Rod.

Michael Lucas was there and apparently was one of the performers on stage (I heard he planned to pee on someone so I skipped the show). I kept running into him all night and he kept looking at me expectantly but I can't for the life of me figure out what it was that he wanted me to say. Earlier this year, his film had swept completely the GayVN Awards and there was much lingering animosity in the porn world. Michael was already something of a lightning rod figure and his blowout was a bridge too far for some. Chi Chi on the other hand was effusive in her praise of Michael on stage. Yes, she was almost too nice, like Robert Blake gushing about his great wife at Vitello's restaurant moments before she got shot. "Did you hear how nice I was to Michael tonight? Tell everyone how nice I was." Duly noted, Chi Chi.

Lucas exclusive Ben Andrews was there in his eyeglasses and hoodie with no shirt underneath. I think Ben has a Superman/Clark Kent thing about his glasses, like somehow no one will realize he is porn star Ben Andrews if he doesn't take them off. Colton Ford was also there, preparing to sing later at the event. I spent a few minutes talking to Colton, and Ben, and it was nice to have a private conversation with them for a change since nearly everything else we have ever said to each other has been broadcast live on the radio. RuPaul was Chi Chi's other guest for the evening (aside from me), but he didn't stay long. He just dropped by to say hi to Chi Chi and then headed home. I didn't even realize he was there until I saw him ducking out of Chi Chi's DJ booth, really only stopping by to drop off some music to Chi Chi. It was too bad because Ru was one of the few people there that I wish I had gotten more time with.

A huge number of those porn star/escort types at the HustlaBall were brought in by Howard from FabScout. I met Howard two years ago the first time we did Fort Lauderdale Pride and I kind of really like him. The pride event was trying to make the whole event more "family friendly" by sidelining the local nightclubs and their hot shirtless bartenders and strippers but they were all too happy to take their sponsorship money. Howard hates that kind of hypocrisy and so do I.

Porn agents generally have a bad reputation. Well, why be so narrow? Agents generally have a bad reputation. Porn performers are consistently and depressingly messed up and flaky. Tonight in the DJ booth Chi Chi and I waxed poetic about the former Gus Mattox and how nice it is to see a hot man who also is reliable, smart and fun. "If only all porn stars could be forty-five..." I thought out loud. Unfortunately most of them are 22, or younger, and don't know what they want to do with their lives yet and don't know what it even means to have a job. So, I don't envy Howard's job (or Chi Chi's for that matter), although he does have lots of cute guys to look at so it could be worse.

One of Howard's boys was a porn star named Riley Burke. Riley is a delectable blond with a thick of chest hair and a willing personality. If given half the chance, I would desert us on an uninhabited island and fuck his brains out forever. Unfortunately, my three and a half year old niece has a better grasp of her own emotional state than he does, and tonight was especially messy. He spent most of the time hanging out with adorable Seth, the "hung Czech" personal assistant, future lawyer, certified massage therapist. Seth has a flawless body, which was on full display during his 20 minute nude massage in the VIP lounge, and he was totally sweet and fun. Not to mention that years of yoga have paid off to the point where he can put both of his legs behind his own head. However try as we might, through hours of hollow banter and empty flirtation, there just wasn't any real sexual chemistry between us. Riley on the other hand, had my attention at all times. One minute sweetly standing with me at the bar telling me his hopes and dreams, the next getting his ass eaten out by a stranger. The munching must have been fantastic because as soon as the guy was done, Riley was unzipping the stranger's pants, barely getting "where do you live" out of his mouth before the stranger's cock went in it. What a lesbian.

Riley's self-esteem was falling faster than prices at Wal-Mart. This made me want to rescue him but fortunately I am old enough now to know what a complete waste of time that is. Riley kept asking Chi Chi, who had directed him in one of his most recently movies, how he looked. It didn't matter how many times Chi Chi said he looked great, he asked again and then caught another disapproving glimpse of himself in the mirror. When I tried to say good bye later, he smiled wanly and brushed me away. Seconds later he burst into tears, surrounded by the comforting arms of two muscle-bound escorts. I guess the evening was just too much for him and he snapped. Riley had said earlier in the evening that he thought Howard was too hard on him, but now I am thinking maybe Howard wasn't tough enough with him. He is a beautiful guy but if he can't pull himself together he won't last six more months in this industry and he'll be dead before thirty.

We left the HustlaBall and headed into a cab. Chi Chi and I were both hungry for a classic slice of NYC pizza. In the cab ride back to her swank hotel none of the pizza places were open, so I volunteered to run to the corner and pick up a slice for her while she got out of those painful heels. Sixteen blocks later and nothing including the all night pizza joint with the sign that said Open 24 Hours was open. Ugh. Doesn't anyone in Chelsea eat greasy food in the middle of the night anymore? Then it started to drizzle. That was the end of that. I love Chi Chi but it's not like she promised me a kidney. I performed above and beyond the call of duty. It was fun, but now it was 2:15 in the morning on a school night! Time to wrap things up. I picked up a couple of sandwiches and a bag of chips and returned finally to Chi Chi's room, where I think she had long since given up all hope of ever seeing me again. My beloved *Postcards From The Edge* was playing on her TV and we bonded a bit more over our shared love of the movie. "I love 'these are the options? Lana, Joan and you?'" Chi Chi declared, quoting her favorite line from one of the many terrific confrontations between Meryl Streep and Shirley MacLaine.

In the car on the way home, I thought about my favorite line from the movie. "Never let 'em see ya ache. That's what Mr. Mayer always used to say. Or was it 'ass?' 'Never let 'em see your ass.'" Tonight I saw Riley's ache and his ass, and I think I speak for everyone when I say, I'd rather see his ass.

Stars Fell On Alabama

Sunday, September 23rd. Someone's friend, by way of getting to know me, recently approached at some night out and said, "I hear you know every gay celebrity." While it is true that I am a shameless name dropper, especially in my blog, it sort of surprised me. When I reflect on my life, it is always the quiet moments that ring out the loudest for me. In biographies, it is the stories of stars meeting stars at cocktail parties and movie sets and the like that pad the otherwise dull adventures of a life lived. But when I think back on my own life's biography, it is rare that a celebrity encounter or friendship leaps out as a defining moment.

I think about the many overnight trips I took driving at night alone from Los Angeles to Salt Lake City, my car winding through the darkened canyons that make up the narrow Nevada/Arizona/Utah connection, dramatically illuminated by my headlights under a starry night sky. It always reminded me so much of *Thelma and Louise*. I think about the dead kittens I found in my barn in Michigan, ripped to shreds by some feral animal, and kneeling alone in the yard to bury their tiny parts behind the abandoned chicken coop. I think about riding the rockets in Tomorrowland with my friend Geoff singing "Fly Me To The Moon" at the top of our lungs. But tonight I think about Danny Roddick.

Recently, it seems that my whole life is centered around porn. The porn stars I hung out with in New Orleans and at the Hustlaball, going all the way back to March when I flew to San Francisco to attend the GayVN Awards. The annual gay porn event honors the best in skin flick entertainment and I was nominated for my non-sexual performance in *Big Rig* for Colt Studio. John Rutherford, who owns Colt listens to the show and when we were first starting out, we had John on along with director Jerry Douglas and assorted stars to promote their new movie *Bucklcroos*. It was a huge, two DVD cowboy epic that John and Jerry co-directed.

While they were in studio to promote the movie back in 2004, a listener called up and asked why it had been so long since there was a trucker porn movie made. John explained matter-of-factly that it was simply because getting the trucks was so hard. The phones lit up like a Christmas tree with truckers offering up their trucks. John directed that movie, called *Big Rig* and offered us parts in the film. I ended up flying out to California to shoot my scene with porn star Colby Taylor and got to know the ever wild Jason Crew in our two hour drive to the location. It was a lot of fun and eighteen months later, I was sitting in the Castro theatre on a rainy night waiting to not win an award for it.

I never really knew Danny Roddick. I met him briefly a few times, most memorably when he sat behind me during the GayVN show that night. He was a Colt Studio exclusive for their Buckshot

Productions line, a lovable nerd boy with the bulging body of a man and we all sat in the same section together. He was making catty gay comments about people that I strained to hear over the noise of the crowd because it was definitely better than most of the show. I don't think he knew I was eavesdropping but I doubt he would have cared. And that was the last time I saw him until tonight.

There was a screening earlier this evening of *Brotherhood*, his last film for Buckshot Productions, over at Jerry Douglas' perfect New York City apartment. Even though we live in the same city, I have rarely seen Jerry since his visit to our studio way back in 2004 so I was pleased when I received an invitation email. When I called Jerry to RSVP on Friday, he said something about "concerns about exploiting the situation with Danny" but I had no idea what he was referring to and I made a mental note to ask him about it tonight at the party.

I drove down to the city and parked nearby on the Upper West Side and made my way to his building, a classic prewar with beautiful original styling. Jerry lives in what is known locally as a "classic six," a six room apartment most coveted by New Yorkers seeking space and comfortable in a real estate market that rarely offers either one.

In what has no doubt been a tradition for decades, the group of two dozen men threw themselves onto couches and pillows tossed on the carpet to watch Jerry's latest film. I thought it might be weird to watch a porn movie in a serious setting like this, but it ended up being weird for reasons I hadn't anticipated. Before the screening, Jerry said a few words, as a director is wont to do at their screening, and it was then that I learned that Danny Roddick was dead. Moments later, there he was, youthful, smiling and beaming on Jerry's TV, as though nothing had happened.

Tonight I came home and decided to look for some information on what had happened. He was so young and it seemed such a surprise. Drug overdose is the apparent cause, although according to some, it was the porn industry itself that took him to the edge and beyond. I don't work in the porn industry so I only know what I have seen firsthand. It's a business, and one in which the performers have a very short shelf life, and I don't mean that in a callous way. Erik Rhodes is right. Once they've seen your pussy (Britney!), what else do you have to show them?

Those who have stayed in the industry for decades have done so because for them it is a career, and not a short term ego boost, an infusion of quick cash, or publicity for their escort business. I don't think the porn industry has a drug problem. I think the gay community has a drug problem. And having the kind of job where you can make a grand in a single day is just the kind of work a drug addict loves: short hours, quick money and plenty of time off. Throw in low self-esteem and you might as well be pouring gasoline on a bonfire.

It would be impossible for me to know every gay celebrity, or even most of them. Not really know them anyway. I spend a few minutes with them talking on the phone or sitting with them in a weird glass terrarium with wires and headphones between us. I gather information, which is not the same thing as knowing a person.

After all, how much do we really know about anyone? Even in our tabloid culture, we still know more about Britney Spears' pubic hair than we do what's going through her mind. Danny Roddick's MySpace page lists "Children: Someday" but that someday is never going to come. It's just too late now.

Maybe I should have turned around in my seat at the Castro Theater, introduced myself, and gotten to know him better but I always assumed he would be on the radio show on that very same someday and I would have gotten to know him then. Then again, Reichen Lehmkuhl and Jenny Shimizu were both on the show on Friday and even after 40 minutes, I can't honestly say I know the two of them either.

I even spent some time with them later in the VIP area at Splash Bar, tucked away behind the DJ booth in an airless storage room filled with bar supplies and some stools. I put them on the spot to spell each other's difficult last names (they both succeeded with flying colors) and did my best to hear them in my deafness as I made the smallest of small talk in the noisy club. But I don't think I understand them any more now than I understand why, among the DVDs and VHS tapes of Madonna videos and camp classics that Splash had a copy of *Schindler's List* on the shelf.

Maybe I will never really know anything or anyone. Even spending a lifetime of writing about myself, who will ever really know me either? I write about the bars I go to and the gay men I linger around town with, but is any of that really the sum of who I am as a person? I hope not.

The late Gene Siskel used to end every celebrity interview he conducted with the same question, "Tell me something you know for certain." The answers would often be something like "I know that I love my children with all my heart." One thing I know for certain: I will never know Danny Roddick.

Lather, Rinse, Repeat

Wednesday, September 26th - It feels like all I ever do is go to Bowery Bar and then write about it on the long train ride home. Ugh! I don't even like that bar and yet it feels like I am there all the time!

I'll admit it. I don't have much of a social life. Not that I really had one before I bought a house an hour outside the city, but it is in even greater disrepair now. It is starting to feel like my weekly Tuesday night sojourn downtown is the full extent of it. Otherwise my days generally consist of:

- me sleeping until almost noon

- eating a bowl of Frosted Mini-Wheats while watching *The View*

- wandering through my new house annoyed by the disrepair but too lazy to address it

- Fucking around on Towleroad.com, Yahoo News and MySpace

- Realizing how late I am from sitting on the internet

- Hopping in the shower

- Driving to the train

- showing up minutes before my show

- Doing four hours of radio which leaves me with no interest in humanity

- Dashing out of the studio to catch the first train home

- Heating up something to eat while watching *Robot Chicken*

- Fucking around on the internet until I realize it's 4am and then going to bed

- Lather, rinse, repeat

This has left me with all sorts of problems. I have a house that needs some TLC. I have no desire to go anywhere or do anything. I have a radio show and a video podcast begging for content (not to mention a blog), and no compelling interest in existing outside of a four square foot area radiating out from my own bed. If I could get away with a bed pan that I emptied out my bedroom window and using a mini-fridge as a nightstand, my dream life would be complete. As a kid I couldn't understand why people like Howard Hughes ended their lives in a single room, but now I wonder at what age I could get away with it without it being totally creepy and crazy. Is forty too young?

Is this what advancing middle age does to you? I suppose this is what it does to me. When I first came out in my early 20s, I would go out to bars almost every single night. Back then my lather, rinse, repeat involved me and my friend Michael Duggan from high school. We would go out all night, eat a pre-dawn breakfast at Denny's and then he would go to sleep and I would take a shower and head off to work at the drug clinic. Then I would race home at 4pm and go to bed. Michael was working as a dispatcher for the Sheriff's department in an afternoon shift. So he would wake me when he got home at ten and we would begin our night out at the bars. Lather, rinse, repeat, kill your liver. I am pretty sure the patients at the drug clinic could smell the booze on me. I was very popular.

Ours was a fun-loving heartless life of carefree nocturnal adventures followed by a zombie-like performance at work. I remember at the time not understanding why people didn't want to go out every single night. It was so much fun! But then again, I was twenty-two years old with an endless supply of energy, living in an apartment with no TV or air conditioning. We didn't have any money but we sure had a lot of fun. And that was the name of the game.

Now that it is almost twenty years later, I have a TV. A big one too. At fifty inches, I am fairly certain that it is larger than the table and chairs we had in the kitchen back then. There's air conditioning and a dishwasher and a big yard backing up to lush greenery. We have video games and the internet and recliners that look like sophisticated leather club chairs. And bars filled with energetic twenty-two year olds who look right past you with a happy blank eagerness waiting for the empty joys to come.

To be fair, the Bowery Bar crowd is really not that young and even in my late 30s, I am still in the appropriate age range. But the bottomless thrill I used to receive on topless dance floors has faded like the ink on a piece of sun-bleached paper. I still go out, but it is mostly out of force of habit than a yearning force of nature. Perhaps it is from so many years as a bridesmaid and not a bride. Now it just feels like you are standing up at the wedding of a friend you are no longer all that close to. But you go because this is where you are supposed to be.

Zach, one of our few ridiculously hot listeners, was in town this week with his boyfriend so I agreed to give them a studio tour and a drink out on the town. He is fresh out of the Air Force and I like to do what I can to support the troops. It's my own version of the gay USO. So I took Zach to Bowery Bar since he is relocating to New York City. He needs to know where to find and converse with the other ridiculously hot people in the city once he gets here, and that location on Tuesday nights is still, eternally Bowery Bar.

It was also a good excuse to finally see DJ Ben Harvey who has lately taken a page out of my book and been something of a hermit while packing and unpacking from his move to DUMBO (the neighborhood in Brooklyn, not the Disney movie, although that would be kind of cool). The stars continued to align with roommate working late and Chip Arndt being in town for the AIDS Ride. I even sent a text message to D-A-N who happened also to be going to Bowery Bar tonight (although I suspect he is always out on Tuesday night and it is not casual coincidence that keeps us running into each other).

Zach only stayed for one drink, but it was long enough for him to swap military tales with roommate. He had a very early flight and a hot boyfriend waiting for him at the Hilton, so he was excused. Ben Harvey was as adorable as ever, and we almost got three sentences spoken between us before the usual suspects began parading through the door like it was a red carpet premiere. First, Peter Stickles, late of HereTV's *The Lair* showed up, this time minus his good friend Michael Carbonaro. Apparently Michael the magician couldn't pull his enthusiasm for going out tonight from a hat, so he opted to stay home. I know the feeling. But since he is 15 years younger than I am (at least), that wasn't excuse enough for me.

Then D-A-N arrived in a red muscle tee and playfully tussled hair. His pupils were like two giant black holes from which no light or tall, strapping lad could escape. Draw your own conclusions. I last saw him downing an orange juice like his throat was on fire and talking with Lance, the formerly straight waiter who abandoned his pussy hound ways to chase men. His resume seemed to intrigue D-A-N when I told him, so when I saw the two of them exchanging numbers on my way out for the evening, I wasn't surprised. Oh and Lance Bass was there and I meant to talk to him because we got offered an interview with him at 11am and I like Lance and NSync and all, but there is no reason for me to reorder my world (i.e. sleeping until noon, Mini-Wheats, etc) just to talk to him on the radio. I was about to go over but they were leaving and I just thought, "Eh. The publicists will work this out, or they won't."

I was wearing my shiny PlanetOut backpack from 1998 because it is easy for others to find me that way and I am trying to bolster their miserable stock price by reminding the who's gay of Bowery Bar that they still exist. This caused me to be spotted by a PlanetOut executive who wondered where I got it then realized that he knew me from FantasyMan Island, my long defunct column. While talking to him, Chip Arndt bounded up to me like a hungry lion with his friend Greg.

Greg is everything gay men and straight women aspire to be: tall, thin, and put together just right. He is the gay guy straight girls are always trying to set up with any gay stranger they meet at a party because they can't fuck him themselves. Chip is sexy and wonderful and I wish he was running for something so I could vote for him. I admire him because when he and Reichen broke up, he let Reichen keep all the fame they accumulated in their relationship. Chip kept his dignity and I suppose a set of dishes, possibly some stemware.

Speaking of dishes and stemware, celebrity party planner Wade Williams wandered in and I didn't even know he was in town. I razzed him about not calling me and insisted that we were now even from when I came to LA and didn't call him, but he insisted it wasn't the same thing. Whatever. I feel even. Conor was also there, complaining about an upset stomach, which caused Ben Harvey to also feel unsettled. I think the two of them make each other queasy. That was the last exchange I had with either one of them. Ben slipped away into the crowd, as did Conor at some point. Finally, I realized that it was late and I had to catch the train home. So I bundled up roommate, kissed Peter good bye at the door and sailed away in a cab.

Usually I like to have some kind of 360 degree connection to round out the story but I don't have a lesson tonight. That would make this story about life out at ye olde gay bar outside my normal cookie cutter structure. Maybe the lesson is that I am in a rut. It's not a bad rut. In fact, I like it very much.

I'll have plenty of time to catch up with Ben Harvey at my housewarming party on Saturday and I'll see more of Chip on Sunday when he returns home from the AIDS Ride. However, it did feel like a wasted night at Bowery Bar and perhaps that is why it is so hard to come up with a suitable ending. I saw most of the same faces. Had the same drink I always have. Hated the same pretentious gays I have always hated. And then came home to eat something fried and watch some TV, which is what I would rather have done in the first place. Lather. Rinse. Repeat.

I may not be living in one room yet, but in my head I am getting pretty close. And honestly, I don't mind.

24 Hour Party People

Monday, October 1st. It is well-established that when it comes to parties, I have real issues. But with good reason!

When I was a kid, I threw a party and no one came. It was just like that scene in *Little Man Tate*, only it was my own fault. We had recently moved to a new town and I didn't invite any of the new kids from school, only all of my old friends who lived quite far away. Not only did none of my old friends come, no doubt because they forgot to tell their parents who would have needed to drive them, but when I showed up at school the following Monday and told my new friends what happened, they were furious. All of them said if I had bothered to invite them they would have come. Stupid me. I have never made that mistake again.

My friend Dennis Hensley also loves to throw parties and I determined early on in our friendship that there were two guest lists that he worked from: the short list and the big list. The short list is made up of his close circle of writers, actors and comedians that he invites over to his condo to watch *Miss Black America* or Tori Spelling TV movies. The ensuing conversations and banter are so amazing, he turned it all into a book and a failed TV pilot called *Screening Party*. Since I coined the term "short list," I am now permanently on the short list. The big list is for things like Dennis's birthday and he basically spends the weeks beforehand passing out flyers and sending emails to every hot guy he knows or meets. The big list parties tend to be huge, popular bashes filled with hot studs and the comedians who love them.

When I throw a party, I am always a big list person. I will invite anyone and everyone to my parties. Unless I hate your guts, you can come. My ex-boyfriend Fat Ass is a shirt stealer. When we dated, he hated my favorite shirt so he asked me to give it to him and then he promptly threw it away. Years later, when he slept with my roommate he stole Mike's favorite shirt too. I know that in science two does not establish a pattern but in this case I think it does because he knows he is a shirt stealer and I can prove it. Years later, when everyone he knew was getting invited to our parties and he wasn't, he sent us my roommate's long lost shirt, I assume in a bid to get invited over. It didn't work. When he resurrects my baseball jersey from the trash, he will be back on the big list, but until then, he's out.

It probably seems strange that someone like me that on the *Star Wars* hermit scale is somewhere between Obi Wan Kenobi (isolated person on a populated planet) and Yoda (isolated creature on an unpopulated planet) would love to throw big parties but I do. I have two speeds: utter solitude and massive party. There is no in-between for me. Those are the only two modes I am comfortable in. Fortunately, this weekend, it was all party, all the time.

On Saturday, I threw a much delayed housewarming party. Well, Romaine has been in her house since December 2006 without a party but to be fair, she did have a baby in the interim. Even still, I moved in the weekend before Memorial Day so waiting so long to have a party is somewhat bad form. I have been telling myself that part of the delay was a need to remodel but mostly I wanted to wait until the crowded summer was over so more people would be available and the weather would be cooler (my house does not have central air conditioning and a party in August would have been murder).

I had an insanely good turnout for the party on Saturday, much better than I would have expected given how far away the house is from all known civilization. But I suspect people wanted to get a good look, cross it off their list, and probably never return. Frank DeCaro accused me of discouraging him from coming and he was very annoyed to discover what a glaring omission he was. Honestly, I didn't think they would all come! And Frank was missed. But he also missed every other party I have thrown for the last four years, so when he didn't make an appearance on Saturday, I was neither surprised nor annoyed.

Romaine came with mother, baby and girlfriend Iris in tow. Iris spent the entire party with the baby strapped to her chest in a baby carrier, rocking back and forth to a classic American Bandstand episode no one else could hear. Cyd and Dan were there in matching grey hoodies, which prompted me to ask them how long into their relationship they starting wearing matching clothes, and explaining to Romaine's mother that the only real reason to be gay is the ability to double your wardrobe instantly.

Fredrick Ford and my old friend Tony were the first to arrive, ironic since they are the newest and oldest friends I have in the city. Tony and I worked together at AOL back in 1947 when it was still called International Business Machines and Fredrick and I met mere weeks ago when he did my radio show for the first time. They were so early that they got to join me on an adventure getting a full propane tank. Who knew that Home Depot sold the tanks empty? No wonder I couldn't get the BBQ to light the first time out.

DJ Ben Harvey was there with Conor of course, along with their cute friend and their other cute friend. Their quartet of cuteness was short-lived and Roommate's now-defunct Friday night geek squad was collectively sad to see them go. They did thoughtfully bring a set of casual matching coffee mugs and a 2008 Chippendale's calendar. I will get some use out of the mugs and Romaine will enjoy the calendar since she has worn out the 2007 calendar we got from model Charles Dera the last time he was on the show. Unfortunately, I didn't get to catch up with Ben Harvey as I would have liked. Nor was I able to get a second to show him my double-sided Ciccone (Six Degrees of Separation from Madonna, as it were), the only thing that could even remotely be considered ART in my house.

As usual, people got stinking drunk. Someone (me), passing through the kitchen, blurted out the recipe for a sex on the beach cocktail and a few gallons of liquor later, the drunkest part of the party (the last to leave well past the scheduled end time) decided to decamp to Manhattan for more mayhem. The party started promptly at 2pm with the arrival of Fredrick and Tony on the two o'clock train and officially ended at a little after nine when the last drunk piled out the door and headed for the bright lights, big city.

Roommate was exhausted by two weeks of non-stop painting, wallpaper stripping and cleaning before the party even began, so by 9pm he was all sharp elbows and clearing throats despite a drunk gay's inability to sense a subtle hint when he is slammed in the face with it. Finally by 9:30pm, the house was clean again and we were ready to head for the cool expanse of the basement to cocoon in front of the new fall shows on my wide screen TV. And then the doorbell rang.

Misreading the 2:00pm to 8:00pm party time as an 8:00pm start time, burgeoning hip hop duo Goddes and She appeared fashionably late at 9:30pm. Not wanting to throw them out after they drove an hour to be there, I got all Pamela Harriman on their ass, cranked up the BBQ and served up more food and polite company for another two hours. It wasn't until Midnight that we finally collapsed in front of the TV for some much deserved mindless entertainment.

Sunday I journeyed into the city to welcome Chip Arndt back from his latest AIDS Ride. A decent crowd had gathered in front of the Gay Center, though it turned out I was the only one there to welcome him back personally. I ran into Cory walking by, he and his friend drawn in like moths at night to the curious gay dance music blasting out of the Center. I can't believe it's already been more than a year since we last saw each other just out and about, when he spotted me plastered out of my mind at Therapy and reminded me that we had already met just a few weeks earlier at *Another Gay Movie*. I honestly hadn't remembered meeting him at the movie, I was so self-involved and also distracted by Michael Lucas, who had encircled me in his cone of gossip on our way out onto the street. But then our brief encounter at Therapy suddenly captured my heart in an unexpected way. Cory, with his Master's Degree in Public Policy from Harvard and straight eyebrows on that granite overhang of a forehead shrouding his soulful eyes, is almost too much for me. That second time we met I was overwhelmed and then a year of radio silence until now. This is going nowhere fast. With my luck, it will probably be another year before I see him again.

Chip's friend Greg was also there, having joined Chip on the ride. Greg, comfortably slim in his tight bike shorts and matching shirt was full of platitudes about my piercing blue eyes; it was the kind of embarrassment I never tire of. Chip and I had a long thoughtful conversation about life and death and in the car ride home I thought how my weekend would have been complete if I had had the same amount of time to just sit with Ben Harvey too. Unfortunately, there is a finite amount of time in a day and in one's lifetime. I always seem to be short of time these days. The never ending story of my laziness versus my grand schemes for life continues. Hopefully, I will finish turning my house gay and have that long, rich talk with Ben Harvey that I always seem to be meaning to have. And maybe I will even see Cory before another summer rolls around. Or maybe I will just lay around the house thinking how nice throwing another party would be, but still reveling in the joy of just being alone.

Little Girl Lost

Saturday, October 13th - A weekend at Disneyland. Rough job right?

Attended Gay Days Anaheim, the coy unofficial name for three days of fun in the Magic Kingdom, with winking approval from Mickey. I like Disneyland. The artifice doesn't bother me. If anything, I find it comforting, which I suppose is the key to their success. The magic's in the clean, careful consistency, the sheer repetitiveness of the images. Alice isn't just a girl who fell down a hole, Disney insists, she is a ride, and a spinning tea cup and a parade float, graphic t-shirt, film on DVD and an opportunity to sing-a-long for generations to come. Sara Lee, Aunt Jemima and Betty Crocker combined can't match the magnificent force of commerce that embodies a Disney Princess ™. The consequence is a total immersion in Wonderland itself, a magical place where wallets open like blooming flowers as busy Disney bees eagerly pollinate.

There were a smattering of listeners who recognized me throughout my adventure, and I stood by warmly, posing for pictures, feeling a bit like a face character (Definition: *a young Orange County teen drafted to physically recreate a mermaid, a fag prince, or a young woman undone by a cursed spindle*). It continues to be the height of silliness that anyone would want my picture, autograph or the chance to sit next to me on a rollercoaster, but for me it beats stuffing envelopes or working in a sewer. At least Disneyland feels like an appropriate venue to act out my childhood fantasies of fame, however misguided or narcissistic they may be.

I say all the time that some people never get over being a twelve year old girl and some people (gay men) never get over not being one. It is such a little girl notion to want people to think you are pretty and stand next to you. Guilty as charged I guess. For a day or two at least. Then I can go back to the four walls of my house where neighbors only care that I remember to mow the lawn every once in a while and lay awake at night wondering how much longer I will be driving that loud car down their previously silent street.

My generation, if I have one Carrie Fisher, is trapped in perpetual childhood. The gays live forever like extras in *Saved By The Bell,* if the new class had never arrived to relieve them of their teen duties. Marriage? No thank you! I just need a date to the prom. Toy collecting instead of child-rearing. I fear the Me Generation has birthed the Me Me Me Generation. Who am I to swim against the tide? Besides, being a kid, for the most part, is a lot of fun.

The downside is how easily your feelings can be hurt when things don't always go your way. Hence the fierce partisanship of the country, frivolous lawsuits (this spilled coffee is everyone's fault but mine!), and truly outlandish public behavior by petulant man-children who, like Disney's Peter Pan, never grew up, but did learn to multitask on planks extended over crocodile-infested revenue streams.

After Disneyland, I visited real live children at my Mom's house, spending a few hours with my nieces and nephew before flying home. In between I planned to attend Dennis Hensley's delightful bowling birthday party. Somehow my intensely emotional three year old niece got the idea in her head that she was going to a birthday party too. When no such party materialized, she collapsed in utter devastation by the front door, sobbing inconsolably. My sister rushed to the kitchen to find something that could approximate birthday cake while I tried to explain to her that she really didn't want to come to the party with me.

“It's for old people.” I insisted, but she was unbowed.

Through tears she declared, “I want to go to the old lady birthday house!”

How do you explain to a three year old that the party in the bowling alley with cupcakes, a coloring book project, and all the licorice you can eat is strictly a middle-aged affair? In a way, you can’t. A Popsicle in her mouth and SpongeBob on the TV and moments later she forgot that I had ever been there, let alone the despair surrounding the never to be seen old lady birthday house.

From the happy confines of Dennis' birthday party, I sped away to the airport for one last thrill ride. Flying still fills me with the childlike wonder that only a barely passing grade in Physics can give you. No matter how many times it is explained to me, I will never understand how that big heavy plane full of people lifts off the ground and travels thousands of miles in a matter of hours. To me it is as magical as the Peter Pan ride at Disneyland.

Perhaps we don't get over being a kid because the unknowing wonder of it all is so much better than the crushing miseries of adulthood. The safety bar can barely keep you in your seat, let alone contain your excitement as you whirl over Victorian London, so much better than regulation coach seats and lopsided exchange rates. You spin past Big Ben as the clock strikes "past your bedtime" as you journey past the second star on the right and on until morning.

If only a Popsicle was enough to calm our adult tears and life's disappointments, but for a $91 park hopper pass and a little imagination, you can get by.

Mark Your Calendar

Friday, October 19th - It was a perfect day in New York City.

I love this time of year. The temperature is a cool 70 degrees, day and night. The trees have started to turn but there is still a flourish of green on the branches. It is so lovely now, but it will quickly come to an end. Soon the holiday crush will overwhelm the city.

My office building on Sixth Avenue will join the festivities with their usual display of outlandishly oversized Christmas ornaments, a corporate staple of the Avenue of the Americas near Rockefeller Center, spurred on by the larger than life toy soldiers that adorn Radio City Music Hall across the street. With fifteen foot candy canes strewn about casually and three foot red glass balls stacked four high in pyramids, the street has the look of a late December living room floor in mid construction. Just half a block away, the massive Rockefeller Center Christmas tree awaits its missing ornaments.

But now the streets are just littered with people. During the day, the homeless are largely invisible, driven into the subways or just around the entrances to panhandle. On the street, business people scurry past the numerous tourists in a frenzied pace, like the squirrels at my house who madly dash about this time of year for nuts to store for the winter.

The intense walking in the city is something that those of us who live there take for granted, but it is often too much for those who are just visiting. The tourists collapse along the sidewalks, unable to keep up with the breadth and width of our great city. Standpipes are for sitting, lamp posts are for leaning. True New Yorkers roll their eyes and brush brusquely past them on their way to Starbucks or other important meeting place.

After the show tonight, I too dodged tourists on the outskirts of Times Square as I dashed over to Therapy where Chris French and company were engulfed in Avalanche, the first mixer of the year for Ski Bums, the local gay ski club. We interviewed Chris on the show four years ago and he is still talking about it. I have been dying to do some ski activities with them, but my work schedule makes weekend trips to Whistler and elsewhere virtually impossible. Even the cocktail events from 7-10pm are largely out of the question. But I figured the alcohol and the boys would still be flowing when I dashed over there tonight and with winter coming, I am making a concerted effort to join in their fun this year.

The first person I ran into is my delightfully handsome friend Mark from Los Angeles. Back in the fall of 1995, I went to work at Sony Pictures in Culver City. The studio was on the old MGM lot and the land also included David O. Selznick's old studio, fronted by the famous "Mansion" so recognizable from the opening of all of his pictures, just down the road. I worked in the non-descript Tri-Star Building, on the far side of the main lot that had once been home to Lorimar, the producers of Dallas and other television programs. Mark worked on the other side of the lot, first in the prestigious Thalberg Building, and then later in the old MGM school house where Judy Garland and Elizabeth Taylor once attended classes between scenes.

Mark was the only person who was ever really genuinely nice to me at that studio. Granted we became friends because I worked in Special Events, so I was the go-to guy for tickets to movie premieres and occasionally good swag, but even after I left the studio, he remained just as nice as always. Once I was having lunch with some other publicity people just outside the commissary. They asked me, if I could work anywhere at the studio, where would I want to work.

"At the Mansion!" I exclaimed, forever in awe of the tremendous Hollywood history under our own feet.

The other motion picture publicists were horrified. "You don't want to work there. They do television there."

The sin of the Hollywood hierarchy. No matter what you do in Motion Picture, it is infinitely better than anything in Television. It is almost as if the more profitable an industry is in Hollywood, the more it is looked down upon. Movie people look down on TV people who look down on Music who look down on Home Video and so on. I never felt that same disdain from Mark, and later when he left motion picture for television and then online, it was only confirmed for me. Whatever. When I heard that Sony paved over what was left of the yellow brick road when they bought the studio, I knew it wasn't the place for me anymore.

But now Mark is living in New York City and it is my chance to return the favor of kindness he showed me so many years ago on the Sony lot. I can introduce him to some of my friends that I think he will like, and probably a potential boyfriend or two. So it was a fortuitous jaunt I took to Therapy, spurred on by last night's fleeting good weather.

Today it is raining, and soon the candy canes will come out of hiding and the snow will fall, delicately covering the stained sidewalks in an all-too-brief splendor. And like the squirrels, I will be burrowed away somewhere for the winter, uninspired to leave my warm nook until the first signs of spring. But for a few hours, it was a perfect day in New York City.

Mall Rats

Tuesday, October 23rd - This weekend, I went to the mall.

I am not really a shopper. I know that some people really enjoy just walking aimlessly through a store, or even a series of stores, in a zombie-like zen state, where "shopping" is a passive experience. This is not me. I don't understand going to a store if you have no intention of buying something or no pressing need. Maybe it was all those years working retail. A store is a place of business to me, filled with busy people, folding sweaters, filling four-way racks and planning floor coverage. It is not a place to linger and leave things in disarray just because you have a few hours to kill.

I only like to shop when I have something I need to buy. I want to walk right into the store, find exactly what I am looking for <u>on sale</u>, make a purchase and go home. No chit chat with the sales clerk. No rummaging around to see what else they have. If I am going to waste an afternoon, I would rather do it in front of the TV or lounging on an Adirondack chair in the yard than under bland florescent lights with chirpy 70s cover tunes droning on in the background.

I was headed out to New Jersey to attend Romaine's post-Baptism party. I tried to convince my roommate Mike to spend his single free weekend day out there with me, but he wasn't having it. He had a list of things to buy and it had a big red Target circle on the top of the list. So I decided it was easier to drop him at the mall along the way, attend Romaine's party for a bit, and then meet up with Mike in the food court next to the Panda Express for some Orange Chicken. It was a perfect plan.

Romaine lives in New Jersey about as far away from me in New York as humanly possible for two people who work so closely together. I suppose I could have bought a house in Connecticut, but why be so unruly? Still, it is a solid hour and a half between us, especially when you factor in a drop off at the Palisades Park mall along the way. When I arrived in the lesbian wilderness, the party was in full, loud swing. The Patterson clan was there, cackling up a storm on the wrap-around porch. Romaine was inside, a serene Buddhist calm about her, spurred by the beer in her hand and the sleeping baby upstairs. And the louder the Pattersons get, the quieter Romaine gets. She is more like her mother than I think she would like to believe.

In the kitchen, Romaine's gregarious sister Sabina was wielding a large knife, scrapping the charred remains off the outside of a large hunk of meat. Apparently, the roast wrapped in bacon sounded delicious, although the barbeque had other plans, igniting the bacon-fat into a beef inferno that could not be put out. Sabina rescued the meat and the meal was sensational nonetheless. Just, like the Pattersons themselves, unnecessarily dramatic.

I made my quick escape from the party and sped back to the mall where an unfed Mike was anxiously awaiting Panda. Parking at the mall was insane. It was like Christmastime, as I drove around in circles for fifteen minutes waiting for a space to open up. Inside, controlled chaos reigned as droves of straight people clustered outside the Lane Bryant, FYE, and other notable retail chains. In a way, the mad melee was exciting, and it is easy to get caught up in the excitement and mob mentality a good mall can deliver. Plus, what is not to love about a mall that has everything you could possibly imagine?

Even though I was stuffed from Romaine's party, I still managed to put away both servings of orange chicken. Egged on by the frenzy of the crowd and the sugar high from my large Dr. Pepper, I even bought a mountable shower caddy and a towel rack for my bathroom. They had been on my own list for quite some time, and I found them quickly in the lavishly oversized Linens 'N Things. The caddy was even on sale! Mall life is definitely not for me, but the occasional visit certainly can have its charms. I just have to remember to not go back before January.

Lotus Entertain You

Wednesday, October 24th - Ben Harvey was back on the show tonight for Tabloid Tuesday. I always like having Ben on because he really tries to stay focused. He came prepared with notes about celebrities and print outs from PerezHilton.com. I came with a bag of carrots and celery and no mood to talk. We prattled on about the history of our show and Ben's recent dust-up with Wade Williams, which I would give about a 1.3 on the Andy Richter scale of celebrity feuds. Ben feels things deeply so he took the Wade thing (whatever it was) personally but every time it gets mentioned five minutes later I can't even remember it anymore.

Ben and I have been anxious to spend some more quality time together, but every time we meet out at a bar there are too many distractions (D-A-N, Conor, etc.) and never enough quiet corners to process like the lesbians we are. So since Ben was on the show tonight, we endeavored to hit the town afterward. Once the show started he sent me a text message about going to Lotus instead of our usual Halloween haunt Bowery Bar. At this point, Beige is as colorless as its name so I am happy to take any other Tuesday night suggestion offered.

It turns out that our quality time was spent on the subway down to 14th Street because once we got into Lotus, it was the usual slew of distractions and loud music. At first, I didn't think I had ever been to Lotus, but once inside the drunken memories of the Sirius party celebrating one million members came flooding back.

My HR pal Calliope had broken her leg and stationed herself with drink in hand in the banquet near the door, passing out car vouchers to the myriad drunk employees so plastered they couldn't even hail a cab. Chinese food was served with chopsticks that had Sirius printed on them. I squirreled several away in my coat and I still have them at home in my eBay box. The biggest souvenir of the night was not the chopsticks, but the heretofore hot straight male co-worker that made out with me by the bathroom. He too was given one of the coveted car passes from Calliope, who even in per prone state, had already heard about the antics before his tongue was out of my throat.

There was no such straight man-on-gay action at Lotus tonight. The usual Here TV posse was there, encouraged to stop in by party host and star of *The Lair* Peter Stickles who was filling in for a sick friend. Peter looked so sexy in his crisp black shirt and pants, pulled together so smoothly he seemed to be made entirely of cream cheese. Peter is smart and knows he can get a lot of smiles per gallon with that devilish grin of his and a well-placed wink.

Chris and Josh were also there from Here and immediately Ben was sucked into the kind of work conversation I know all too well from hanging out with co-workers at bars. I let them have their office gossip while I chatted with my friend Terry and his new young squeeze. Occasionally Chris would swing through with some titty-twisters from hell, that I was fortunately spared. My nipples are for show only, and any attention, even just looking at them, causes nothing but pain. I was ready to shatter a glass on the edge of the bar to prevent Chris' hand from coming anywhere near my chest.

At one point I started talking to Hunter, a product placement expert, who strategically placed himself in the dead center of the bar for maximum exposure. He looked so familiar and I was fairly certain I have seen him before on Connexion (although hours later I realize he just looks like my friend Brandon's ex-boyfriend Cliff). We talked for all of two minutes before someone took the stage and announced the beginning of the burlesque show. That was my cue to leave.

I could barely hear Peter over the dance mix of Heat Wave a few minutes earlier, so I knew I didn't have a chance during a live performance. A topless girl twirled glittery fiddle-covered nipples to *The Devil Went Down To Georgia* as I left for the midnight train to suburbia. At least Ben Harvey and I had a few minutes to talk about our lives before I grabbed my old PlanetOut backpack from coat check and headed for a cab. Maybe next time we'll just have lunch instead. The lighting is harsher but at least you can get a word in edgewise.

And for the most part, people keep their nipples to themselves.

Bitter Gay Men

Thursday, October 25th – My birthday is on Sunday and it is hard to hide my irritation. I tried to talk about it on the air the other day and I just don't have any words for how I feel about my impending birthday. Why is 38 such a flashpoint for me? Perhaps it is the dangerous proximity to forty. I have been joking that 38 is the new 55, and I really am starting to mean it. Because, in the gay community, you can get old, you just can't get older.

If you go out to an event or a gay bar and you see an eighty year old guy, it's sweet. The gays will buy him a drink and hear about the time he saw Judy Garland perform live at the Palladium. But if a 42 year old guy walks into that same gay bar, it's sad. Doesn't he know when to quit? It's not a gay sin to be old, but it is downright criminal to grow older. And where are the gay men in their 40s and 50s supposed to go? They can't all hide out in Palm Springs until the Social Security checks start to arrive. But when I look around, increasingly I am the oldest person in the room and I start to wonder what will happen when the dot on my palm turns red and I need to run.

Hanging out with Terry Goldman and his new squeeze, ten years his junior, we got to talking about gay men who get older and turn bitter. Earlier I had spoken to Lucas Entertainment exclusive Ben Andrews, with his 22 year old skin and 11 inch cock. He had just returned from the Lance Bass book party and saw Debbie (excuse me, Deborah) Gibson there. "I didn't even know who she was." he admitted, "Except, you know, what I saw on VH-1."

No surprises there, except perhaps the idea of someone so young watching Vh-1. He was still in diapers when she danced on the sand with a denim jacket sliding off her shoulders and a scrunchie in her hair. When Reagan died, my ex-boyfriend Sean, who was born at the end of his first term, told me that he didn't know until that moment watching CNN that Reagan had been an actor. "They never taught us that in history class." It's enough to make anyone over the age of 35 contemplate suicide. Or the survivors turn bitter.

Terry started in on the interns at work, who when he told them that there wasn't internet when he was a kid, looked as surprised as if he had said he didn't have electricity or indoor plumbing. He tried to explain what a BBS was and they looked at him like he worked his way through college delivering ice from a horse-drawn wagon. "Don't tell them you didn't have your first cell phone until you were almost thirty." I urged him, and then prompted him to ask his new guy if he had ever been to a Fotomat.

Remember the Fotomat? That was one shit hole of a teen job. I still shudder when I think of those kids with nothing but a transistor radio and some comic books to pass the time inside the familiar A-frame structure. Even before digital, the Fotomat was an arcane dinosaur, with the Polaroid camera coming out of the sky like an earthbound comet to wipe them off the face of the planet. Now even the Polaroid seems quaint. And this is where the bitterness comes in.

I have said many times that you know you are old when you start talking about places that don't exist anymore. I never appreciated the song *Come Up To My Place* from *On The Town* until I got older and realized I could also rattle off an old guidebook full of destinations as distant to twenty-something gays as the Hippodrome is to me. No wonder you feel like the party is over, the place where they used to hold the party closed years ago and now it's a condo complex. I would say internet café, but even those are fading into the ever rapid distant past.

My mom has a theory about why it seems that time speeds up as you get older. While waiting for your birthday between the ages of four and five, a quarter of your whole life has to pass to make it to that point. But when you are going from 50 to 51, it's only 2% of your life. It turns out (in a move that defies the laws of physics) that the more you accumulate over time, the faster you travel. This might explain why so many people retire just so they can sit in one place, not moving, for extended periods of time. The world is just travelling so fast at that point, there is nothing you can do but just hang on. Which leads me finally to the wisdom of Tennessee Williams:

"What is the victory of a cat on a hot tin roof?" Brick asks Maggie, their empty life together at a crossroads, on the eve of Big Daddy's final birthday.

"Just staying on it, I guess. Long as she can."

Alive For Now

Monday, October 29th - Well, I passed another birthday and nothing horrible happened. A few years ago, while doing a Google News search on myself around this time, I discovered I was dead. A man with my name in England (there are apparently many) was murdered, but nothing makes you more confident growing older than seeing yourself dead. This year, another Derek Hartley in England didn't die, but he was missing! I have been anxious for weeks hoping I would be found safe and alive, not dead in a ravine somewhere. Then, on Monday, he was found alive, starving, and somewhat mentally ill. Thin and crazy? Sure beats dead!

Originally, I had planned to join some of the gang from work at Six Flags today. And as much as I love a rollercoaster (and using my season pass), it just didn't feel like how I wanted to spend my birthday. Roommate works Sundays now and I shoved off any real birthday celebration plans to next Saturday when I wouldn't have to compete with Halloween. Being born three days before the notorious holiday, my mom has often joked that if I had been born three days later she would have named me Jack O'Lantern. Except I don't think she was kidding.

Last night, Roommate and I hauled our old selves down to Manhattan to see *The Kingdom*, which wasn't nearly as bad as the miserable box office and tepid reviews would have you believe. It was directed by actor turned director Peter Berg, whom I have had something of a slow burn crush on since Linda Fiorentino grudge fucked him in *The Last Seduction*. He was also quite frequently naked (especially for a ski movie) in his big break movie *Aspen Extreme*. If he could spend twenty minutes of that movie stark naked in the snow, I think the CW can find a few minutes for those *Supernatural* boys to shower off.

After the movie, we decided to take the late drunk train and have a quick drink before we left town. We wandered down to Barracuda, which was packed to the rafters with gays. It wasn't so crowded that Terry Goldman didn't find me. He kissed me and his lips tasted like strawberries, like he was wearing lip gloss made for a nine year old girl. But he tasted good, so who am I to complain? But we immediately decamped from the madness of Barracuda and made our way to the relative quiet of XES, somewhat around the corner.

During the summer, I forced Erik Rhodes and his fabulous boyfriend Danny to meet me there for a quick post-show drink. They live not far away and they thought I was joking at first that there was even a bar at that location since apparently their dog has crapped outside it a thousand times without them noticing it. Once inside, Danny still thought I was joking, but the upscale dankness and casual neighborhood vibe I think won him over. Then again, it was the last time we went to a bar together, so maybe he thinks my taste is permanently suspect.

While at XES, I had my usual sex on the beach after first checking my look in the mirror. I spent a few minutes staring at myself in the bathroom mirror, reviewing the merchandise and giving a buyer's assessment of the bill of sale. Not bad I thought, for something that has been in the bargain bin for so long. Mike and I parked on stools, transfixed by the horribleness of a shitty horror movie playing on the flat panel TV over the bar. We decided it was probably *The Hills Have Eyes* since it was terrible, just terrible, and neither of us had seen it before. The sound was muted so we had the distinct pleasure of reading the dialogue as it scrolled across the various dismembered performers. The screenwriter clearly loved movies, as the internal movie references were seemingly endless, and I wondered why, if he loved movies so much, that he had inflicted this particular piece of garbage on the world.

While wrapping up our drinks, a listener, who had recognized me, came over to wish me a happy birthday. This is extremely rare in NYC and, as has been the case in the past, he was originally from Miami but had recently moved to the area. He was very nice and I will be honest that it did make me feel good, almost like a real celebrity, on my birthday. But the drunk train was calling and we beat a hasty retreat.

Once home, I couldn't fall asleep. It was already several hours into my birthday and I considered just not sleeping at all for the entire 24 hours. I spent a fair amount of time wading through the seemingly endless birthday wishes emailed and posted to MySpace, corresponding with the adorable, argyle-loving Jack Mackenroth, stars on his elbows and in his eyes as he awaits the upcoming season of *Project Runway* and texting at 4am with an ex-boyfriend actively sorting out his emotions after a break-up earlier in the evening. Then, I decided to watch *Mrs. Miniver*, which I had DVRed from TCM.

I haven't seen *Miniver* in 20 years but I had remembered it fondly. I was struck however by what a horrible performance Greer Garson gave in the movie. Her bizarre expression rarely changed and she seemed to be Acting with not just a capital A, but also with lights around it and a brass band. But you have to love MGM at the height of its power. There wasn't a close-up where she didn't look like a million bucks waiting for change. Teresa Wright was terrific and it seems crazy to me now that she could have been in three of the biggest classic movies of all time right in a row (*Miniver*, *Shadow of a Doubt*, *Pride of the Yankees*) and then had very little else to show for her career from then on out. The movie itself was a good story to watch on a birthday and in the midst of a war. An important reminder that life is short and at all turns unexpected, but there is still time in between bombing raids for a flower show or a little romance.

It was well after dawn that I finally threw in the towel and went to sleep. Promptly at 11am, my cell phone started to ring with calls and buzz with text messages. Wisely, my mother waited until 7pm to call. "I didn't wake you, did I?" I barely had the heart to tell her I was just up from a nap. Whatever. It's my birthday.

So what if I puttered around the house, hammering on the keys of the piano trying to learn *I'm Old Fashioned*, trying to meet the neighbors by hand-delivering some misdirected mail (they weren't home), and grilling up dinner outside in a parka for likely the last time of the season? No one said you have to celebrate a birthday in only one way. I like being alone. And having the house to myself on a beautiful fall day to wander around in my underwear and eat ice cream was just what the doctor ordered.

Gay Life Exposed

Wednesday, November 7th - Yes, I am possibly the gayest person alive. But for me, being gay is something of a hobby. I enjoy it, but I like to think I can't make a full time occupation out of it. Then again, it's a little bit like being a die-hard Yankees fan. It doesn't matter what career you may pursue, everyone assumes that most of your waking thoughts are about baseball. I wish there was a way to leave the unfinished puzzle of my gay life on a game table in the living room and run some errands unrelated and unfettered by the lack of resolution. After all, it will still be there when I get back. But as gay people, we are vertically integrated by not just our love of sex with men but also a desire to arrange flowers, listen to Judy Garland or declare someone too fat for that outfit. As much as you may want to quit, hide or sideline it, gay can pour from your pores like the smell of gin from a notorious alcoholic.

Apparently, for some people, gay isn't just a hobby, it's a way of life. And for them we have the Gay Life Expo. These kinds of expos are like speed dating between gay consumers and mainstream corporations. In each case, they are hoping to find perfection. But just like most speed dating rounds, what actually stands in front of you can often be very disappointing. For the gays: disappointment in the quality and diversity of the companies that bothered to show up.

For the companies: wonder as to the location of these high end consumers demographers have been promising them for years. And if you ever want to dispel the myth of gays as fashion forward, articulate trendsetters, this is the weekend adventure for you! Other myths, such as gays being indiscriminant whoring drunks and lesbians being aggressively cheap and demanding of free items, remain woefully intact.

I wanted to go because I think it's important for our company to crack into the NYC gay market in a substantial way. And a trade show seven weeks before Christmas is as good a place as any to plant the holiday gift seed. It was also a chance to spend some time hanging out with co-workers that I like (Jeremy Hovies, Keith Price) without the embarrassment of needing to be nice to the ones I don't like, which I will have to do soon enough at the annual holiday party.

I had a short segment on the stage that I originally thought was just an opportunity to wave to the crowd and throw some free t-shirts to the lesbians. But when I was at the office thirty minutes before the show printing out the information, I noticed that I would instead be an emcee and be introducing some of the performers. This was not good news. Emceeing at a pride event is hard enough, but at least the crowd is drunk and excited. Performing at a trade show is like trying to sell real estate to death row inmates. The chairs are usually filled with people too lazy to walk the length of a convention center without needing to rest an hour for every ten booths they passed. I tried to encourage them to enter to win the free radio we were giving away, not more than ten feet from the closest chair but most of them preferred to stay in their seats and stare dead-eyed ahead. I don't need a TV show now. I already know what it feels like when people watch you on TV, from the perspective of the television set itself.

The lowest form of degradation came at the end of my set when Scott Nevins launched into his "game show" with the OutQ personalities playing along with "real people" from the audience. Scott, with his Groucho brows and pancake make-up projecting like Ethel Merman to the third balcony, took to the stage like a rat diving into a sewer.

For the purposes of the game and a chance at some playful nastiness in my direction, he paired me with a genetic male cross of *Ab Fab*'s Edina Monsoon and Jodie Foster in *Nell*. He was wearing X-Ray goggles from the back of a 1970s comic book and a puffy white jacket with the entire NYC subway map printed on it, his native language that of Leeloo from *The Fifth Element*.

It seemed from his insistent waving of a gay bar rag in my face that he was in the current issue of HX Magazine, photographed for Halloween in what I can only assume is his normal attire, and captioned as "Bee Bitch." So the other hosts had actual contestants and I was paired with a lump of mashed potatoes. As I should have learned from the Faggot Feud with Richie Rich in 2004, never walk on a stage where someone else is controlling the mike. Point taken.

After the event, I decamped with the folks at HERE TV for dinner. Cutie pie Chris was there again, although in retrospect, I realize he was the only actual HERE person at the restaurant. At the Expo, I saw Josh, but he opted to head home after the long weekend and crash. Earlier from the stage, I saw Peter Stickles walking around, but he left before I was unshackled from the umpteenth just-so Judy impression emanating from little Scotty Nevins. I hope Peter didn't see me, but as a performer, I am certain he would have sympathized with my plight. Lady in a cage!

So it was Chris for dinner and my friend Terry from Los Angeles. The other two were flirty Jimmy with sad eyes and a boyfriend in a steam room (unrelated) and adorable newcomer Jonathan, who was too young to appreciate my dusty early 80s references. Hey, did you know that Vic Morrow was named Rotary Club Man of the Year?

What? Too soon?

We went to Ariba Ariba, which in the absence of real Mexican food, will do in a pinch. Jonathan and I bonded over our mutual hatred of the sexy yet slow homos who were occupying our future table. Besides, we were in a hurry. I noticed in the midst of the football game playing on the TV over the bar that the *Amazing Race* was starting that night and I was fairly certain it wasn't in the DVR at home. There were 3:34 minutes left in the third quarter which I gay-estimated was about an hour left in the game. With an hour of *60 Minutes* sandwiched in between, I knew I had to leave as soon as the game ended to be home in time to not miss the start of the show.

It turns out Jonathan is as plugged in to politics as I am, and he is in the midst of reading *The Nine*, which I have been dying to pick up. I am such a Supreme Court junkie, I would call in sick to work just to watch a televised confirmation hearing. Then again, I would call in sick to eat a container of ice cream, so the threshold there is pretty low. And I was enjoying all of our banter until I looked up and noticed the football players touching each other inappropriately and CBS announcing the Play of the Day. In my head I heard the stopwatch ticking and Leslie Stahl, with her whipped cotton candy hair and dulcet tones, laying out her segment about famine in Africa, Lindsay Lohan or both, and I knew it was time to go.

As I raced home through the wooded splendor of the Saw Mill Parkway, the concrete monoliths of Manhattan in the rearview mirror, I took stock in the level of gay in my own gay life. Years ago, I left the ghetto behind. I loved my time in West Hollywood, but a body can only take so much abuse, and really that kind of stress testing is for the young. My existence now is suburban, surrounded on all sides by the known markers of heterosexual existence: soccer moms and RVs. And in the middle of it all, my little Cape Cod house, with the bay window and stocked bar in the basement. It's as gay as a picnic basket, even without the bags of flower bulbs waiting on the window seat to be planted, carefully arranged by blooming season and selected to resist the voracious dietary habits of the deer that cruise my yard like it's The Ramble.

In looking over the goods presented at the Gay Life Expo, I don't think my life, as defined by their terms, is gay. Yes, I am fussy about my few precious elegant things, but I think that is borne more out of a desire for strict traditionalism and less about homosexuality. I'm old-fashioned, and I don't mind it, as the song says. But given how unlike the rest of my family that is, I suppose I can lock that final piece in my gay life puzzle and consider it solved.

I'll Take Manhattan

Friday, November 9th - I never look at the weather before I leave the house. It's a terrible habit I picked up while living in Los Angeles. In LA, the weather just never changes. Today's weather report in Hell: 72 degrees and sunny, just like every other day. Sure, there are a couple of rainy days in January. But just looking out the window you can tell what the weather will be like for at least the next 48 hours. Besides, everyone drives. So even if it does rain, everyone has an umbrella (along with a sweatshirt and rollerblades) in the trunk just for emergencies. In fact, the flat line weather is such a cliché in Southern California that Steve Martin made it a significant plot point in *L.A. Story*. It is for this reason that I was caught unawares by the rain in Manhattan tonight on my way home.

Earlier in the day, when I was frantically tearing the house apart looking for my iPod so I could rip Britney's terrific new CD into it, I noticed my umbrella sitting on the sideboard in my dining room. It came into focus as if a piece of crucial evidence in a Hitchcock movie: a folded newspaper on a motel room nightstand, the flicker of a lighter in a pair of eyeglasses, and now my umbrella lying dormant under a window, a cloudy sky foreshadowing in the background. But I ignored the umbrella to pursue my missing MP3 player. It turns out the iPod was in my backpack all along, right where my umbrella had been until I tossed it out after wearily carrying it around for two unpredictably dry months.

Today I wore my favorite grey wool coat that I picked up last fall at the Barney's Warehouse Sale. It is a short, fitted jacket that makes me feel like one of the Von Trapp boys in *The Sound of Music*, my tribute to Gwen Stefani and her *Wind It Up* video. Unfortunately only an old sheep dog smells worse wet than a wool coat. So I ran as quickly as I could through the rain, Britney's ridiculously hot *Toy Soldier* song urging me along, as I wove a delicate race between umbrella-carrying tourists and the dangerously slippery metal grates strewn about the sidewalks like land mines waiting to fell the unsuspecting with their cruel slickness. Diagram that sentence, bitch!

Britney and Los Angeles were both on my mind as I ran from Rockefeller Center to Grand Central Station. Earlier in the day, Michelle Collins emailed me to let me know that she had quoted me on her *Best Week Ever* blog. Yesterday on the show, she was raving about Britney's new album, although with the caveat that it was processed to the point that on some of the songs she sounds like Gwen Stefani. After hearing *Toy Soldier*, I said that it was as "processed as a Kraft single." Michelle couldn't believe that I made it up in the moment and expounded on the theory (even further in her blog entry about it), perfecting it for the audience. Her rabid enthusiasm drew me to the Virgin Megastore after the show last night to experience Britney's collective *Blackout* for myself. And Michelle is right. It is good. Arguably, the best Britney album ever, especially given how utterly shitty most of her work is.

I will be in Britney's adopted town of Los Angeles this weekend. I read on PerezHilton.com that she has a new Mercedes SUV, which is good to know. If I see one coming, I will pull over immediately, like when an ambulance is going by. I am in town for my high school reunion. It's been just over twenty years since I walked out of that school for the last time. It is strange for me to be going back this week since it is also the twentieth anniversary of my lost virginity. What does one give as a gift for that anniversary? A shop-worn, empty box?

All I really care about is looking better than everyone else who comes to the reunion, which is the only reason to go. I remember Cindy Crawford bringing her *House of Style* crew to her ten year high school reunion and thinking that there is no finer revenge, or better use of a television crew. No doubt her former classmates ran around telling everyone what good friends they had been with the supermodel, only to have those lies ripped to shreds right there on TV for everyone to see. Cindy confronted all of the popular girls who had been so mean to her, and cornered the boys who had refused to ask her out. And she killed them with kindness, a brand of torture porn the makers of the *Saw* movies could only aspire to. People were more relaxed at the Nuremburg trials. Cindy is my hero.

I don't have a camera crew to follow me around, nor do I have a TV show. It is unlikely that anyone in my suburban LA high school would be impressed with my lowly satellite radio career. It's not like I am in the movies or something, as most of them doubtlessly are, even if it is below the line. Then again, I still look pretty good for my age, mostly the product of vanity, no kids, and lots of product. I have a cute suit to wear and I am approximately the same weight I was in high school. Unfortunately, there isn't anyone from my school that I care to torment. I wouldn't mind seeing the guy I lost my virginity to. And our pompous class president. Neither of them came to the ten year reunion. Oh well. At least I will get a meal out of it, and a long weekend in Los Angeles. I hope it doesn't rain though. I already packed nothing but shorts and t-shirts, and true to form, I didn't bother to check the weather.

Down The Rabbit Hole

Thursday, November 15th - It seems like I am always running late. I don't know why time consistently slips away from me, but the older I get, the more it seems to evaporate before my very eyes. Over the years, I have had jobs that have barely required me to show up at an office, let alone at a specific time. I used to joke during my years at America Online that I worked dry cleaning hours: In by ten, out by four! Even that was an improvement in structure after working from home for two years. Since coming to SIRIUS, I am required to physically remain in one place during very specific hours. This has been the hardest challenge for me. I just don't know that it is in my nature to be on time.

I was watching a documentary a while ago about Marilyn Monroe, a woman notorious for being horrendously late. She apparently arrived at her last photo shoot before her death only two hours late, which was early for Marilyn. When she sang for President Kennedy, Peter Lawford introduced her as "the late Marilyn Monroe" an irony brought home weeks later when she died. During the shooting of *Some Like It Hot* a few years earlier, she was eight hours late to the set. Director Billy Wilder was exasperated but not surprised. "I got lost on the way to the studio," she declared of the studio lot she had worked on for more than a decade. I figure as long as I am never that bad, I am money ahead.

Last night after the show, I had agreed to attend a *Project Runway* premiere party, hosted by my new friend Jack Mackenroth. The TV show started promptly at 10pm of course, which also happens to be the exact moment my radio show ends. So it was physically impossible for me to travel from my studio in midtown Manhattan to Greenwich Village in the blink of an eye. I warned in advance that I would be late, but even still. It just seems so like a diva to stroll in late for a live show. Especially when claiming your own celebrity as the excuse for such bad behavior. But it is the nature of the beast.

It also happened to be the last day of work for our show producer Dan. I entreated everyone to not have the going away festivities on that night because I knew I wouldn't be able to stick around, so that is exactly when they scheduled them. So then I got to look like a complete douche running out on everyone. But when you live a story, I guess people around you want you to live it too. Consistency, however annoying, is more important than perfection.

The party was in a converted carriage house and I must say it was a delightful living space. NYC is the best place to go for unusual homes and I was most impressed by how simultaneously modern and antiquated the place was. When I arrived the door to the street was wide open and a hundred attractive men were squeezed into the upstairs watching a flat panel 70 inch screen on the wall. I made amazing time, arriving just 20 minutes into the show, but still, I was too late to mix, mingle, or talk to Jack Mackenroth. I watched the show there (and again when I got home), and I am definitely looking forward to this season. However, I hated most of the clothes. Just blah. And Jack's model walked like a lumberjack carrying an axe uphill. Jack's dress was cute, a perfect Barbie ensemble, that I half expect closed in the back with a large metal snap at the neck. But then, Lumberjack Barbie started trudging down the runway and I thought he should have swapped out her sexy purse from Bluefly.com with a nice redwood log.

While the show was going on, a cute guy named Ben started up a conversation with me. Even though it was slightly less crowded the further you got from the TV, we were both pinned fairly close to the dining room table without much room to move. Naturally, I used this opportunity to help myself to two of everything. And since I was so far from the TV and already missed some of the show, there didn't seem to be any harm in talking to a nice young man for a while.

Ben was adorable with a rocking body and, despite my eating like a hungry wolf in front of him, we seemed to be hitting it off. Then, Michael Lucas met my eye and started over toward me, a regal push through the crowd. "Do you know Michael?" I asked. Ben let out a declarative bleat and beat it on the lam, blending quickly into the crowd.

Michael was in rare form, air kisses and broken English enveloped us like perfume. He lifted his shirt several times to show his amazing abs, which were quite impressive. It must be hard in the winter time to have a sensational body and have to hide it under so many layers. His abs popping out made me sad that I love ice cream more than physical perfection, but then I remembered that I get to eat ice cream and no one has to see me naked in order to have a career.

It turns out that Michael and Ben had shared an awkward moment earlier in the evening when Michael introduced himself and Ben reminded him that Michael had fucked him three months ago. "I did not remember him," Michael purred as he gazed at Ben's perfectly formed back from across the room, "but then I saw his ass and it all came back to me." I have to admit that Ben did have, in jeans, one of the most perfect asses I have ever seen. "He also has a huge cock" Michael assured me, his head nodding carefully in approval.

Moments later, lurid creep Baby Chic entered the party which caused Michael Lucas to bristle like he had just wandered into a smoldering dump. You may recall that Baby Chic tried to molest me and Ben Harvey at Vlada some months ago, while Ben was trying to make nice with John of the famous Biscuits and Bath Johns. I remembered Baby Chic's clammy hands all too well and did everything in my power to escape his clutches. Michael and I parted company and I think he was more successful at getting away than I was since seconds later Baby Chic was grabbing my chest as I pushed my way through the kitchen. I was trying to meet Jack but his adoring fans had him completely surrounded and pinned up again the stove. He didn't seem to mind at all.

Jack is so pretty, and as one of the contestants pointed out on Project Runway, he looks like a superhero. He seemed to be in his element last night, a gorgeous tipsy doll swirling through a glamorous party of attractive men and waif thin girl models. We chatted in the kitchen and in the melee he introduced me to the other contestants from the show. It was fun to meet all these people just at the beginning of fame, not after they had already been cast aside by the cruel fate of reality television. Jack also pointed out a beautiful blond model named Megan who had been on America's Next Top Model, although during that reality stint, she was Meg, the rocker chick with the brown hair and bold-faced attitude. She was giving us full tilt Grace Kelly though as she slipped away from the crowd and down the stairs.

Unfortunately, my own time at the party was drawing short. Even though I am late all the time, the train home to the suburbs doesn't wait for middling radio personalities, no matter what their reputations. So I made my good bye to Michael Lucas and to sexy Jack Mackenroth. I tried to say good night to Ben but I think my obvious friendship with Michael Lucas had tainted me for him. He was in the midst of a conversation about fisting with a sexy blond named Chris, who like me, had not had sex with Michael Lucas. Ben related a tale of fisting a guy once, pushing down, down, down, finally getting in up to his mid-forearm.

"There is an artery right there and it sort of squeezes around your hand tight and you can feel their body. It's so intense."

That was my cue to leave. I love intensity in life as much as the next person. But if I want to feel blood racing through an artery it's because I am in a panicked dash through Grand Central Station trying to catch my train home to Normal Town, USA.

Judge and Jory

Friday, November 16th - It seems lately like all Ben Harvey and I do is rendezvous at Vlada. We are like a bad sitcom. On TV, the characters always converge over and over in the same public locations, mostly because it's just cheaper that way. Fewer sets to build. But in life, we imitate art more than we would like to believe. Hence, another Thursday night spent at Vlada with Ben Harvey. At least I am not haunting Beige so much anymore, so that is a plus.

We were upstairs tonight. There is a second bar there across from the DJ booth, but while the bartender is always friendly, they don't have the same selection of infused vodka there. At the main bar downstairs, the tight-shirted men safely behind the napkin stacks and lime wedges can tap whatever infusing jug you like, but upstairs you have to depend on whatever is handy. Since I like a bloody mary with the pepper vodka at all hours of the day or night, I prefer being downstairs. But I love Ben more than vodka itself, and since he wanted to be upstairs, upstairs we went.

I love Ben, and not just because he looks like David Anders the actor who plays Adam/Takezo Kensei, the blond warrior from feudal Japan on NBC's *Heroes*. It isn't even because he also works in radio so he understands the crazy world I live in. We even have a shared love for Rosie O'Donnell's brief but heavenly stint on *The View*. But that isn't it either. I love Ben because he is like a delicious piece of blond peanut brittle: sweet and crackly and impossible to believe that anyone could be allergic to.

Our intention is always to catch up when we see each other, but it never works out that way. He is one of the few people in the world that I genuinely care what happens to, so I am interested in the various adventures of his life. But we always meet up in public places infused with gay men and vodka. The distractions are legendary. Upstairs, it was Jory, the hottest property tonight at Vlada. His form-fitting, wrinkle-free heather grey t-shirt and low slung jeans casually draped over his exquisite body were a siren song no one could resist, least of all me.

His physical form said lifetime of athletic endeavors instead of the usual gay combination of steroids plus too much gym time. His Roman nose and crisp haircut set off his model-perfect looks to a tee. He looked like a man. Not in a gay vs. straight way, or even in a masculine vs. feminine way. He just looked like the ideal embodiment of man in its purest form, like a paper doll ready to hang your fantasies on.

I saw Jory and immediately had no interest in him. Obviously I was fascinated, and studied him in the kind of detailed fashion one might expect from a serial killer. But sexually, it just didn't do it for me. He was like a crazy hot version of Charlie and I was once again a gay anthropologist observing from a distance.

To me, a guy like that belongs on the arm of someone who is: famous, equally hot, wealthy, or some combination thereof. I could never think he was interested in me, and if we were together, neither would anyone who saw us.

I did however think he was perfect for Ben, based on nothing more than his seemingly flawless physicality. I am not even certain Ben was as convinced about him as I was. However, he has the wholesome and squeaky clean look that Ben seems to like, and the notorious matchmaker in me was dying to make some magic happen. I did everything short of overturn a table or shove Ben into him, but it was to no avail. Jory couldn't see past his own eye lashes. He made no eye contact with anyone outside his own small cadre of devoted admirers, and even then, seemed constantly waiting for a better offer to arrive.

My roommate Mike was also there tonight and on our walk to the train we openly mused about what it must be like to be someone like Jory. Mike thought he ignored people because after a while it is just so difficult getting hit on all the time. I thought he might be almost blind like my adorable former intern Patrick, who was exactly like Marilyn Monroe in *How To Marry A Millionaire.* Patrick even asked me if his date was cute once at Bowery Bar (he wasn't), and then politely made his escape into the crowd. If I was meeting him out, he would call me on my cell phone as he was walking in the door, so we could find each other. With his blindness and my inability to see through all the flashing distractions of a bar, we could otherwise be in the same nightclub for years without ever meeting again.

Whatever the reason, Jory was in his own class and his own world at Vlada. In a way, it's kind of a shame. Yes, Mike is probably right; it would be a burden to be so attractive. But if he didn't want guys hitting on him, he would get fat and wear a loose-fitting sweatshirt with a stain on it, or take down that shirtless Facebook photo of himself strumming a guitar. No, no. He likes the attention he draws and I am fairly certain that he was hoping Prince Charming might walk through the door and carry him away. Too many Disney movies I think. It's the curse of the gay community: So many princesses in need of rescue and too few princes to ride in and save the day.

Ben is a prince of a guy, but I wish someone would ride in and rescue our nascent friendship. Tonight was my fault because I was instantly distracted by the shiny newness of Jory. But this is the rule not the exception. Six months in and we can barely get into the meat of anything before one of his friends or mine drops by, and before you know it, he is tired or I have to be on the train. Maybe we just need to start meeting in non-gay places, or at the very least not a bar.

Living outside the city, this is one of the rare opportunities I have to feel connected to the gay community but ironically the circus atmosphere is hindering it at the same time. Everyone wants to be the belle of the ball, but midnight comes so quickly.

Jeopardy Hot

Saturday, November 17th - Sporty Spice (Cyd) and Dental Dan (Dan) had their annual autumn party tonight and I never miss it. Cyd and Dan are a dream couple, the kind of storybook relationship tailor-made for TV news profiles and conniving bitches hell bent on home-wrecking. After all, the only thing the gays love more than a hot man is someone else's hot man. With Cyd and Dan, you get two for the price of one. Anyone wishing to break them up (pay attention Charlie) would be barking up the wrong tree, as they are as right for each other as any two people I have ever met. Plus, they are the perfect party hosts.

When I ran into Mark Levine at Therapy last month, my first instinct was to drag him to Cyd and Dan's annual event. They know virtually every attractive thirty-something guy in Manhattan, and a new man on the scene is bound to find lifelong friendships and at least a few exes at the Autumn Party. I also endeavored to bring Ben Harvey because he had wanted to meet Mark after the tireless cheerleading I have done on his behalf, as well as Cyd and Dan, who he encountered briefly at my housewarming party lounging in matching sweatshirts on Adirondack chairs in the back yard while basking in the afterglow of cheese-filled hot dogs.

Ben, Mark and I met up on a familiar corner in the heart of Chelsea before dashing through the forty degree weather. Despite my legendary reputation for shorts and t-shirts under all circumstances in Los Angeles, I don't fuck around with the cold in New York. I arrived bundled up in my snow parka, looking like an arctic explorer. Ben looked adorable as always and deceptively dressed in light layers over thermals. Mark, still getting used to winter again, just threw on layer after layer until he seemed sufficiently protected from the elements. Once at the party Mark started stripping like Gypsy Rose Lee, which only served to endear him to everyone. By the time he left, he was down to just a clingy t-shirt and jeans.

As usual, their elegantly appointed apartment was packed wall-to-wall with sexy gay men. In the spirit of diversity, a sprinkling of women decorated the otherwise masculine turn out. Cyd and Dan had tirelessly decorated with genuinely adorable fall decorations, virtually invisible to the increasingly intoxicated homos struggling to make eye contact and work up the courage to talk to guys they had seen in the same apartment time and again, party after party. One of those men, Sebastian, cornered me in the kitchen to ask if I was the one who had left the clever response to the eVite in which I said I would be hanging out with Dan in the VIP Room (which in this case was the bedroom, for the Super Bowl party it's the kitchen).

Generally their parties are so crowded; I tend to gravitate to the least crowded location, which is often where I find Dan.

It was all going well until Cory walked in and turned out to be the most pleasant surprise of the night. I last saw Cory at the closing ceremonies for the AIDS Ride, where I was cheering on Chip Arndt. I have written before about his eyebrows and his granite forehead, but it has been so hard for me to fully describe him. I think his face most reminds me of that of the Statue of Liberty, the only national icon I share a birthday with (sorry Julia Roberts). I have always felt a certain kinship with the lady in the harbor and I guess it spills over to Cory. His Masters Degree in Public Policy from Harvard is just the icing on the intellectual cake.

We talked about life and politics (he is just about to move to DC to take a new job) and it was a total delight. By quite some measure the longest conversation we have ever had and it was as rich as I thought it might be. When talk turned to *Jeopardy*, he too had noticed Alex Trebek's flirtation with one of the college contestants. I then introduced him to the concept of being "Jeopardy Hot" which is a man who is hot entirely in the context of being on Jeopardy. Outside the nerdy confines of the popular game show, he would just be of normal attractiveness. But when you watch geek after nerd doling out the questions, a Jeopardy Hot guy is a welcome sight. Mike and I use the subtle distinction of Hot and Jeopardy Hot in conversation all the time, as it comes in handy constantly.

After three parties in a row as the last one left in Cyd and Dan's apartment, I was adamant about not making it four. The party thinned out like hair in a Propecia ad and I hastily rounded up Cory, his friend Jeff, and Ben to continue our fun around the corner at Barracuda. Mark had already gone home, as had 95% of the partygoers, so I knew I had to strike while the iron was hot. Moments later, we were again packed like sardines in a sea of gay men, trying to get a drink at the bar. In between half listening to the hot 80s hits playing in the background (*Major Tom*, *Neverending Story*, *Hazy Shade Of Winter*), Cory and I continued our in-depth conversation about my favorite subject I never get to subject my radio audience to: politics.

Since Cory is from Iowa, I grilled him about the current political climate there. I am always curious about first-hand accounts and Cory was ambivalent about the candidates, a state of mind he also attributed to the rest of the state. I have been riveted to the debates and the tightness of the race, especially among the Democrats. Unfortunately, Cory wasn't able to resolve it for me before he ran home for the night. As usual, it was my cue to leave as well. The damned drunk train was calling again, as it always is.

I left Ben in the capable hands of his cousin Christian, who had met us all out at Barracuda, and dashed off into a cab to Grand Central. Two nights in a row of going out has taken its toll on me, and I can't wait to climb into bed. It's the weekend and a chilly one at that. I look forward to a party of one, relaxing in my living room, far from the roaring seas of gay men, the political fray of Washington and most importantly, the leering glances of Alex Trebek, where the only Hot I need to worry about is the heat from the crackling fire in the fireplace.

Party Delayed, Party Denied

Wednesday, November 21st – The year is nearing its end and that means autumn is almost over too. Gay nightlife is past its peak and already winding down as another brutal winter forces everyone to stay in for the foreseeable future. With Thanksgiving, office holiday parties and Christmas on the immediate horizon, the opportunities to see and be seen are rapidly drying up. Maybe it is too soon in a year to throw in the towel, but with only six weeks left in 2007 I must admit that I haven't been very successful in the projects I have started.

I bought a house which I love, but it has wrought havoc on my social life. Instead of going out for fun, I am forcing myself out on the town just so I don't turn into one of those sad old people who is found buried under a stack of newspapers after the smell wafts out of the house. Yes, playing Scrabulous on Facebook with Jonathan from the Gay Life Expo is a thousand times more fun than having so guy spill a drink on you in a crowded bar, it is a chilling substitute for an actual social life.

I became friends with Ben Harvey and what started out promising disintegrated when Rosie stormed off *The View* and it hasn't fully recovered since. I really like Ben and enjoy spending time with him one on one, but maybe as Carrie Fisher wrote in *Postcards From The Edge*: "We're designed more for public than for private."

I hadn't heard from D-A-N in a couple of weeks. We had lunch at elmo, which I thought I had never been to before, until I arrived and like most places in the world, I had been there many times (including Perez Hilton's 2005 birthday party) but hadn't remembered. The lunch was nice but, as often happens when we hang out, I couldn't tell if we were hanging out as friends or just on a date that never seemed to go anywhere.

I kind of blame myself for this. There were several circumstances, like the night he drove me home, where if I had wanted some kind of answer to the question, I could have made a move. But as attractive as D-A-N is, I don't know how attracted to him I was. So I suppose I just ended up doing the same thing I always do in these situations: nothing.

After lunch, I had walked him to the gym where he was going to work out after eating. This seemed strange to me, but his body is better than mine, so I will have to trust his judgment on this one. On our way through Chelsea he was very excited about his upcoming flight training in New Hampshire that would get him one step closer to his goal of being a pilot.

Two weeks later, he returned from New Hampshire and invited me to a party. You know me, always ready to meet strangers;

though I am trying, after seven years of living in New York, to expand my friend base to a more reasonable size. Read: more than three. Plus I was curious to see where things were not going between us. But then D-A-N got sick and we rescheduled for our usual hangout at Bowery Bar on Tuesday night where I expected nothing more than more of the same.

I arrived at 10:45 but D-A-N was running even later than I was. “You are probably used to that from me by now,” he told me when I saw him later, and as a chronically late person myself I was full of forgiveness. Fortunately, I ran into Charlie, scoping the place for hotties with his lawyer friend Evan. Charlie was lamenting that it wasn’t very crowded (“It’s like a Thursday here.”) which I chalked up to the plunging temperatures. Bowery Bar is a fair weather friend. As the crowd began to thicken like so much turkey gravy, Charlie noticed unhappily that all of the guys outside were smoking.

I tried to explain that they were outside because they could smoke and it was too cold outside for anyone who didn’t need to be out there to be out there. My logic did not satisfy him in the least and he dismissed my explanation with a stern yet youthfully unlined expression. I turned my attention to Evan who was my kind of guy (which means he laughed at all my jokes). Charlie would occasionally wend back into the conversation with a query when he heard Evan laughing, but as you know, nothing improves a joke like explaining it. Even then, Charlie greeted my stories with the displeasure of possibly missing his future ex-husband just to hear my uneducated musings on depraved indifference as debated on Law & Order.

Mike arrived from work and soon Evan and Charlie slipped into the crowd in hopes of finding some non-smokers to attend to briefly but vigorously. At that moment, I spied Ben Harvey's co-host Dave Rubin as he walked in. He saw me too and slowly made his way through the cluster of gay men to join me under the searing heat lamp for a brief conversation. There is just something about that Dave that makes me want to do dirty, oh so dirty, things to him.

Most guys, I see them and like Dennis Hensley has often said, I just want to roll a ball back and forth on a floor or splash along the shore with them in an Amy Grant video circa 1990. But something about Dave, the intensity of his gaze, the firm brow, his sexuality so casual in its roughness, that makes me want to tear his clothes off and toss around like pudding wrestlers. His cadence and square jaw are straight out of Dashiell Hammett, and who in their right mind wouldn't want to fuck the shit out of that?

The literal grilling under the heat lamp was too much for Dave and he had to return to his friends. As we embraced, I finally spotted D-A-N. So after our finally farewells, I headed back inside into the more temperate warmth of Bowery Bar. D-A-N was there with his usual cadre of friends. I liked Pedro the best because, like

Evan, he laughed at my jokes. D-A-N was wearing a tight t-shirt as usual and cut his hair a bit shorter, although his dashing superman swirl is still intact.

Hanging out with him in public is so difficult because he is always surrounded by a devoted fan base. He seems to be the homecoming king of Bowery Bar so it is hard not to feel like you are on the receiving line. Of course it was even worse for Mike, who ran quickly from the melee of muscles to find a nearby perch. So being a good friend, which I generally am not, I left D-A-N to his autograph signing and hung out with Mike.

We talked about the crowd and Mike related an overheard conversation from a balding 25 year old who had insisted to his friend that the guy cruising him was too old for him. "He thinks you are his age, that's why!" I blurted out, Karen Walker spilling from me after only one rum and coke. I also spent a great deal of the evening making snide comments about all of the tweed caps that seem to be in fashion these days. Some of the highlights included: "Somebody loves *Newsies*!" and "Hey boy. Perchance have you the *Saturday Evening Post*?"

D-A-N wondered why I had wandered away so I told him I was trying to be a good friend to Mike. That caused him to decamp from his dark corner and drag his hot guy posse out into our neck of the woods. He tried to engage Mike in conversation but Mike was in Buckingham Palace guard mode and D-A-N was instantly thwarted.

Really all D-A-N wanted to do was fucking dance, but Bowery Bar tossed a new set of banquets into the center of the room making unlawful gyrations even more difficult than usual. He tried to get me a drink but once again the evening was cut short by that pesky drunk train home. I love my new house upstate but what a kill joy it is to have to go home at 1am, even if it is a school night.

Whatever. D-A-N had plenty of men to keep him warm and I am sure if he started to dance hard enough, the crowd would make the space for him. No one likes to be the one to stand in the way of a hot guy having a good time.

And speaking of hot guys, Conor was there too. He had friends with him as well (I only remember the names Michael and Eric because every gay is named Michael or Eric). But my time with him was oh so brief. Stationed close to the bar so his hand was never empty for long, I only saw him in passing on my way to the bar for a refill and off to the bathroom to complete the cycle.

Conor is off to Boston for Thanksgiving tomorrow, and soon D-A-N is off to Boston to fly away for good. But in the meantime, we can pass like drunken ships in the night around the iceberg known as Bowery Bar. It is already too late in the season for that outdoor venue, so it is probably for the best that we are all packing it in for the time being. But why not one last drink?

Jingle Balls

Saturday, December 1st - I am a double Scorpio with a Gemini moon. This is my way of excusing my intensely private nature. Even though I have spent the last decade writing about my life and half that time talking about it daily on the radio, there are still vast aspects of my life I prefer to keep to myself. In the finale of *Six Degrees Of Separation*, I find my life's thesis. I too am not interested in reducing (and thereby diminishing) every aspect of my life to a witty anecdote, parsed out at luncheons and swank cocktail parties. But in this case, I am willing to make an exception because I am an inveterate storyteller and can't pass up the opportunity to tell what I think is a particularly entertaining tale about myself, no matter how personal it might be.

A few weeks ago, I was in the throes of another birthday. I don't relish getting older, but as my mother has always insisted based on no evidence whatsoever, it beats the alternative. So it was in this mindset that as I was soaping up carefully in the shower, I found a lump in one of my testicles. Normally, I am a vigorous sudser, working myself up into a lathered frenzy. But just days earlier I had strained my back while aggressively shampooing (still better than the alternative? I wonder) so I was trying to be a little more cautious. In my lack of haste, the lump became apparent and right there in the shower the end of my life flashed before my eyes. Cancer! Balls chopped off. Chemotherapy. My beloved hair in clumps in my hands. If Sweeney Todd had left a straight razor in my shower, I'd be dead right now.

Hurried scans through webmd.com and Wikipedia assured me that even if it was cancer, it was 95% curable and likely would only require one of my balls to be chopped off. In this case, I mused, it would beat the alternative. But since I live in the world of worst case scenarios, I prepared myself to hear six months to live when I saw my doctor a few weeks later. I scheduled an appointment as soon as I could but in the meantime, I did have a previously scheduled dermatology appointment. So I figured, one doctor was as good as another in doling out the bad news. So when my dermatologist asked "Is there anything else?" I happily journeyed outside his specialty with him and encouraged him to rummage around in my junk like it was a yard sale and see if he could find anything worthwhile.

My dermatologist, ever a good sport, obliged my mania and felt me up. He groped behind my left testicle and felt what I felt. He opined that it was probably nothing but that I should keep my appointment with my regular doctor and have him run some tests. The following week, I was in my regular doctor's office, my underwear around my ankles, my junk on display again. This time, my doctor had real difficulty finding specifically what I was freaked out about. He said he felt a "fullness" but not a mass, which he suspected was not cancer. Besides, he assured me with all late 30s of me hanging out for the world to see, that testicular cancer is a cancer of the young and therefore probably not a worry for me. So he ran some tests and gave me a referral for a scrotal ultrasound and a visit to the urologist.

I know that some men guard their genitals like they are state secrets in a time of war. Personally, I have never understood the notion of being pee shy. Yes, it is annoying when you are trying to urinate in a gay bar and some guy leans over so far you start to know what a drinking fountain must feel like. But as a rule, if someone wants to see my cock and balls, what do I care? I am perfectly content with them, so have a look. It's not like I haven't been looked at before.

When it comes to disrobing for doctors, I am even less shy. In order to work successfully in retail, you have to take the attitude that the money changing hands is not the same as the money in your wallet, and I imagine genitals are the same way for health care professionals. They dispassionately count it out and put it back in the drawer, like a bank teller in a white coat. This attitude was seriously tested however at the ultrasound.

First of all, since it was an ultrasound, I journeyed to a women's clinic and naturally was the only man sitting there. Having seen plenty of medical shows, I knew how an ultrasound worked, and I imagined that running that wand over my balls would be a fairly zippy procedure.

I was directed to a small changing room where a shorty pink robe awaited me. I changed and dashed across the sterile hallway to the exam room. Being nervous always activates my already weak bladder, so the second I laid down I had to pee. But it was already too late. I had to just go for it and hope that I didn't accidentally pee all over myself in the midst of the exam.

The ultrasound technician was a very nice young black woman and the first woman since being a baby to manhandle the goods. She was very dignified about it, casually draping a large paper napkin over my genitals and directing me to slide it up over my stomach so that my penis could be simultaneously covered and pulled out of the way.

I described my lump and where it was and then she set about to map my reproductive system like a cartographer. She squeezed the gooey ultrasound gel on my balls like ReddiWip. The wanding went on for what seemed like forever, and on top of wanting to pee, I also had the desperate urge to fart too, which I knew would be the height of rudeness with her hand on my balls. So like my terror, I held it all inside while I tried to read her blank expression for sudden signs of cancer discovery.

Her expression never changed and after twenty minutes of mapping she asked me to point out directly where the bad lump touched me. I pointed it out and she went over it from every angle.

"I am just going to show your film to the doctor and then we should be all done." She declared dispassionately and left me alone in the room.

Moments later, a nice Asian lady who looked to be about 14 years of age came in and announced that she was the doctor. She told me that she had looked over my ultrasound but was still unclear about the location of this lump I left.

I rummaged around in my junk like it was a disorganized handbag trying to find what I was looking for. The gel made grasping any part of my balls slippery work, like trying to rescue a panicked bird from an oil slick. In my fevered attempts, I had significant trouble finding it myself. I tried staying on my back, then moving onto my side, and finally, standing up. At this point, I abandoned all hope of dignity and just let my junk swing in the wind as my hand molested my ball sack.

"I am not crazy. I know it's in here," I insisted, filled with panic that she would now think I was some kind of weirdo that got off on exposing himself to the ladies in a medical setting.

We both looked at the monitor together. "That's your testicle" she told me, pointing to an egg shaped pale mass. I marveled at what a perfect oval I had, which temporarily distracted me. There was a sea of darkness next to it. "Those are blood vessels over there. It seems like you just have a lot of blood vessels, which might be what you are feeling. It is not uncommon to have extra blood vessels it is just unusual that you just now noticed it. But we will send off the results to your doctor in the next four days and he will go over it with you."

"Big blood vessels," I thought as I put my clothes back on, gingerly trying to avoid getting the gel that was all over my hands and balls on the rest of my outfit. Maybe I had a blood clot in there and at some point it will travel from my balls to my brain and give me a stroke! Sometimes you don't even need to consult a doctor or the internet to get crazy ideas.

So I will see my urologist and my regular doctor in the coming weeks and likely will hear that the only issue with my balls is a lack of symmetry. Not the worst thing that ever happened to anyone. As usual, the worst things in my life are happening in my own head and my genitals are merely supporting players in the larger drama of my life. But I guess it beats the alternative.

Puttin' On The Ritz

Monday, December 3rd - I am a hermit. But I look like the party planner from Sears compared to my roommate Mike. Mike never likes to leave the house, nor does he like to meet new people. Two weeks ago when D-A-N tried to engage him in conversation he did his best impression of a cigar store Indian and D-A-N beat it on the lam. I don't think his boyish charm is used to such a stoic rebuff. So when Mike announced earlier this week that he had been invited to a party, I campaigned like Tracy Flick for him to attend.

Apparently some of the guys from work were having a "So Bad It's Good" holiday movie party. Being the forceful encourager, I naturally had to attend the party as well, thus guaranteeing Mike would go. Plus, ever since we stopped working together, whenever Mike talks about life at the office, I feel like he is describing a favorite TV show on a channel my cable company doesn't offer anymore (Seriously FiOS, why no MSNBC????). Unfortunately, median ages dropped like an anvil in a Tex Avery cartoon since I left the company four years ago, and I walked into the youngest group of people I have seen since a high school class toured through Sirius Radio last month.

It was a straight party, which was for the best. It is bad enough looking across the room and seeing a cute guy, it's worse to think he is precisely half your age. At least in a room full of straight people, I could just concentrate on the bad movies at hand and not worry about my libido.

We walked in during the finale of *Jack Frost*, a cheesy horror flick about a serial killer whose DNA accidentally bonds with snow and turns him into a murderous snowman. The effects were about on the level of a third grade play at a very nice public school.

Once the film was over, we watched 60 minutes of classic TV show intros as an intermission before the next feature, along with some remodeled intros from a heavenly site called FatalFarm.com (*The Facts of Life* is my favorite, followed by *Cheers*, but honestly they are all pretty terrific).

In many ways, it was like attending a party in the future. The house had computers hooked up to the TVs and everything ran off the Xbox 360. It was Hollywood's worst nightmare of copyright infringements gone amok, but I have to say, it was all so delightfully easy.

The second feature was *Silent Night, Deadly Night* about a sweet boy named Billy who becomes convinced that Santa Claus is a killer doling out death to the naughty. Later, he grows up to be a sexy, troubled teen, who when forced to play Santa in a wildly overstaffed corner toy store, assumes the identity himself and goes on a murderous rampage. Along the way, we learn that no one owns a bra and nuns are pretty useless. Hilarity, as they say, ensues.

The film stars Robert Brian Wilson as the sexy deranged teen (an actor last seen in an episode of *Jake and the Fat Man*). His shirtless moments refocused my libido away from the sexy teens at the party and his wilderness of a hairy ass in his one complete nude scene reminded us instantly that this was 1984, no matter how futuristic the party was otherwise.

The movie wasn't *that* bad, although the filmmakers clearly had a massive hard-on for *Psycho* and borrowed liberally from the plot and shot list. The budget of the movie however was so low that at one point a woman refrains from breaking a storefront window to escape because they clearly couldn't afford the replacement cost.

After the party, Mike and I left to find Jonathan, who had been in Brooklyn, but by then was partying it up at The Ritz. I had never heard of the bar, at first thinking he was texting me from the recent revival of the stage show *The Ritz*. But in my defense, Jonathan sees a lot of Broadway shows and it has only been open for six months, which is fast for me to discover a hip new place.

We walked in to the familiar strains of Salt N Pepa doing *Push It* while an early twenty-something crowd giggled with oldies hits delight. At the bar, a fifty year old balding man in a fuzzy short fur coat and rings on each finger clutched a glass of red wine while ogling the bartender's exposed torso.

"That's me in five years." I whispered in Mike's ear, although his askance glance told me it was closer than I thought.

From across the bar, I spotted the back of Jonathan's head moving toward the upstairs. I pushed through the twinks and made my way up the narrow staircase and greeted him in the calmer oasis of the second floor lounge.

Jonathan had already been drinking all night and his "Frak Me" t-shirt seemed less a come on than a declaration of sheer exhaustion. We chatted once again about all of our favorite shows, which is easy to do since we love all the same shows. In fact, I have yet to find anything that we don't agree on. He is even excited about my Friday night murder ladies (aka ABC's *Women's Murder Club*). The show has been called *Sex and the City* in a morgue but it's more like the episode of the *Golden Girls* where Dorothy solves the murder mystery, but with expensive shoes and a winter color palette.

I implored Jonathan to search YouTube for stray clips of my childhood love *Partners In Crime* and sealed the deal with an anecdote about stars Loni Anderson and Lynda Carter wandering into a San Francisco theater and being mistaken for drag queens. We laughed. We shared a Coke and the belief that Diet Coke makes you fat. I think in that moment, I realized that I might be falling for him.

It turns out that Jonathan lives mere steps away from the straight party we had attended earlier in the evening. And even though it was out of the way, since we were parked right outside The Ritz, I assured him it would be no trouble to give him a ride home. It is freezing outside now after all. And the journey back downtown allowed Mike and I to be once again in the vicinity of the Taco Bell on 14th Street.

Unlike earlier in the evening when ye just joked about abandoning hope and all entering here, at 2am we did just that. Along with *Battlestar Galactica*, *Veronica Mars*, and *Arrested Development*, Jonathan also shares our love of the bell and a pair of grilled stuft burritos and a soft taco later, we were back on our way downtown.

Jonathan safely dropped off, and our greasiest cravings sated, Mike and I headed back up into suburbia. Okay, so maybe the party didn't help either of our social skills. We could have stared at a bad movie just as easily at home and skipped the BBQ chips they served. But we did visit a new gay bar. True, Jonathan is already over it, citing its inconsistent DJing, capped by a 30 minute long version of *Gimme More*.

But we ventured out of our comfort zone and down into the secret world of social people. So that has to count for something.

Besides, it was the last night before the snow comes, and there will be time enough for hibernating now that winter is officially here.

See Or Be Scene It

Sunday, December 9th - Jonathan invited me to a party in his apartment tonight. His sister is in town (the one whose face he appears to be licking in one of his Facebook photos) and since she is under 21, he decided staying in to party would be a much better idea. Since it is well-established that we both like all of the same things, he felt it was safe to invite me to a *Harry Potter*-themed party in which we would play *Scene It* (the Muggles edition) and other fun board games. Since I will take any excuse to hang out with Jonathan and I am highly competitive when it comes to games of all kinds, I was happy to sign on for the adventure. I even dragged Roommate along because I didn't want to him to feel left out or spend the evening home alone on a Saturday night.

We sojourned down to the city and descended on Jonathan's apartment with a regifted bottle of champagne (One of <u>five</u> in my house that no one will ever drink) and a plastic container of 23 store-bought bakery sugar cookies with holiday sprinkles on them (one of them accidentally fell into my mouth while bored in traffic on the West Side Highway). The cookies were a big hit and I am sure Jonathan will find a good home for the champagne this holiday season.

If I may veer off on a non-sequitor for a moment... I still don't understand champagne. I have never really been wild about the taste of it (although I am also not a wine person so I am probably not the best judge). It seems fine in mimosas, but a mimosa isn't the kind of drink you can have six of. Really you just have one.

The problem with champagne is that it is a commitment issue. Once you open the bottle, you have to finish the whole thing. You can't just put a cap in it again and file it away for later, like a trusty bottle of gin. And given that it is an alcohol that can only be sipped and not chugged or downed in shots, you really need to have something of an enthusiastic crowd to even bother to open the damn thing.

For all these reasons, I hate champagne. It is the devil. I hope Jonathan likes it, or passes it along because I am certain now that champagne has become the 21st century version of the Christmas fruitcake.

Jonathan was already half in the bag when we arrived, which is just how I like a man. We are so alike, I suppose I shouldn't have been surprised when I discovered he also throws a party in the same way I do: unnecessarily intensely. Like Robert DeNiro sweeping dirt into a dustpan. So much anxiety over nothing. I wasn't there five minutes before he said, "Are you going to sit down? You just standing there is making me nervous." I felt like I was having an out of body experience. It's a dull cliché but he literally took the words right out of my mouth.

We settled in fairly quickly to a deeply nerdy game of *Scene It* devoted entirely to *Harry Potter*. I think I would enjoy (and would win handily) in a regulation game of *Scene It*, but although I liked the films, I only saw them once, never read the books, and really couldn't remember any salient details that might have helped me out in this immediate circumstance. In between, there were plenty of jazzy conversational bits about other pop culture phenomena and I was right in the mix with all of those. A discussion about an upcoming version of the *Veggie Tales* on the big screen led to my best line of the night:

"I thought after the Terri Schiavo case, the Christians were done with *Veggie Tales*."

It got a mixed reaction from the crowd. Maybe it was too soon. After all, my comparison a few moments later of Courtney on *Survivor* to a Holocaust victim went over like classic Don Rickles in Vegas, so it was definitely a group that appreciated more daring material. Jonathan laughed heartily at all my jokes, which is all I really ask for in life.

Terry was there as well, although he was anxious to escape the house party at a reasonable hour and hit the bars. Roommate sat out the *Harry Potter* game and tried to enjoy whatever was happening on the TV screen while also desiring to join Terry in his planned escape from the fun. Unfortunately, Terry wanted to go to Barracuda, which I have previously established is a cluster fuck nightmare now that I am just too old to deal with anymore. I am convinced that one of these nights, just like the mythical rat king on *30 Rock*, a knot of gays will become so entangled in their own egos and drama that they will be unable to pull away and will just have to fight each other to the death to escape.

The *Harry Potter* portion of the evening over, Terry Goldman bailed to meet up with people who were still interested in getting laid on a Saturday night. The gaming at Jonathan's then turned to something much more up my alley: *Namesake*.

Jonathan had raved about this game before when he first invited me over for the party. He had played it in the past and loved it so much, he found one on eBay (it is out of circulation) and bought it. In the game, much like the early scene in the movie *Go* where the checkers battle each other to name a famous person whose name starts with X to decide who will work the cash register, players must name famous people in a series of categories with particular first names.

Jonathan's entire pop culture canon can be perfectly summed up in his illuminating examples for the name Ethel: Ethel Mertz, Ethel Merman, or Ethel Rosenberg. *Namesake* could be the new gay version of the Rorschach test. I'll tell you a first name, and you tell me the first famous person that comes to mind.

I loved the game because it was right up my alley. My brain is like a dusty attic filled with old, broken pieces of pop culture just waiting to be brushed off and displayed on the front lawn for strangers to bid on in a mixture of shock and wonderment. Roommate on the other hand was in a new circle of hell. It was all the things he hated most in life: socializing with people and being put on the spot about pop culture. Plus, the TV was tuned to endless episodes of *I Love New York*, a show that represents everything he can't stand about the darkest low points of his beloved TV programming universe.

Unfortunately, the structure of the game play and general intoxication made the experience last for hours longer than necessary. It is always a bad idea to play board games with drunken people. They have no sense of time passing, which is always a problem, and their slowed reaction times can make something as simple as picking up and reading a card off the board take ten minutes.

At two am, perilously close to the end of the game anyway, there was a general movement to call it quits and head home. It was getting late, and my earlier off-hand suggestion of Taco Bell was looking more and more necessary. Jonathan was also in the mood for making a run to the border, so he closed up his party and joined us on our fourth meal adventure.

The Taco Bell on 14th street is open until 5am on Saturday nights and by 2:30 when we arrived the scene was in full swing. The crowd was almost entirely straight, and a mix between drunk twenty-somethings needing a greasy bite and teenagers with nowhere else to go. I suggested to Roommate that it would make a perfect video podcast. Fourth Meal: A Late Night Soap Opera. So much drama was played out between bites of Chalupas that you wouldn't need to do much more than set up a camera and start shooting.

Jonathan and I engaged in a deep conversation about the shared sitcom structures of *I Love Lucy* and the *Golden Girls* (did you know they both shot on the same sound stage? True!) while, to paraphrase *The Remains of the Day*, Roommate put his thoughts elsewhere while we prattled on endlessly.

And then, just as soon as it began, it was time to call it a night. We dropped Jonathan off and made our way back out of the city. Okay, so Roommate didn't have the best time but tonight was just the way I like it. And it was nice for a change to be at a party and not spend the whole evening worrying if everyone had enough to eat or drink. Jonathan said once that he thought he would be me in a few years. Having seen how he throws a party, I think he is already me in far too many ways. But I don't mind it, if he doesn't.

I Fall To Pieces

Thursday, December 13th - Years ago, when Romaine and I first started working together, she introduced me to one of her great loves in Manhattan: Pieces. The shoebox of a bar hosts a legendary karaoke night on Tuesdays that is something of a drunken staple. As we were getting to know each other, we would drop by occasionally after the show and I would sit back while Romaine would belt out a favorite country tune, her trusty leather jacket on, a bottle of beer in one hand, the microphone in the other. As time went on, we went to fewer and fewer bars together and my Tuesday nights gravitated to hot boy central at Bowery Bar. Flash forward a few years and in need of somewhere new, I headed instead to somewhere very old.

Hot listener Zach, who recently relocated to New York, wanted to hit the town and had initially suggested Bowery Bar. During his last visit to the city, I took him there on a hot summer night and I suppose he just assumed it was hot every Tuesday night. But Bowery Bar has seasons, which is part of why it has remained the hottest Tuesday night in town for more than a decade.

Spring and Fall are the best times to go, weather-wise, and during the summer, when most gay New Yorkers spend their weekends out of town, Bowery Bar is a perfect weeknight opportunity to regroup and exchange notes. But in winter, the giant outdoor patio all but abandoned, Bowery Bar is off the radar, and brave New Yorkers disperse to neighborhood bars that are easier to navigate to in the midst of an ice storm.

I shot down the idea of Bowery Bar and suggested instead that we hang out in a fun midtown bar, conveniently near my office. I wanted Jonathan to join us too, but after spending his entire long weekend with his sister in midtown, he was anxious to explore another part of the city, one would assume in close proximity to his apartment and/or the late night Taco Bell on 14th Street. So I suggested our long ago haunt Pieces. Even though singing was anathema to each of us, it seemed like a fun environment to have a casual drink and pass judgment on strangers. And really, what more do you want in a bar?

I suggested we meet at the studio and head down together. Jonathan had never heard the show so he came an hour early to share in the "magic" as he called it. He settled down in Romaine's usual chair on the other side of the studio while Romaine ran the board. Almost immediately, he pulled out a crossword puzzle and started in on it with his usual intensity and an ink pen. Occasionally, he would chuckle or look up and smile when the show caught his fancy in one ear, but soon he would return to the trials of down and across as we ran out the clock on another show.

As we were walking out, we gathered Zach from the main lobby and the three of us headed for the One train to the heart of the West Village. Along the way, Jonathan and I traded off as tour guides and New York historians, tossing in our own experiences into the mix to give it some humanity. Most of it, like the location of the Stonewall Inn, was already well-known to Zach and, with the temperature dropping, we hastened our walk to Pieces.

The bar was just as I remembered it. The narrow entrance was Tailhook Convention-style cruising. The right side given over to the stage and the devoted sing song regulars. The left side, running the length of the bar itself, was for fresh meat, like us. We immediately took up our position near the stage but decidedly in the fresh meat section.

Earlier Jonathan and I had been buzzing like gay hornets about *Xanadu* and the disappointment that the slim country vignette from the finale was cut from the soundtrack recording as well as from the new Broadway show we had finally seen together, but Zach was ready for a meaty political conversation better suited to *Hardball* than gay bar. Jonathan is a political animal like me, so he was happy to pile into the fight. We discussed electability and the fascinating mysteries of the Iowa caucus system.

All the while, Zach was chugging, CHUGGING gin and tonic. As the drinks disappeared he became more and more adamant about mobilizing Jonathan and me to a higher political calling. He is recently out of the Air Force and I think just getting out of the military is a little bit like just coming out of the closet. He is filled with years of pent up gay with a capital “G” energy and he can’t wait to translate it into action now that he no longer has to look over his shoulder. Jonathan and I, much longer in the mix, are far more comfortable with the current state of affairs. But I admire Zach’s pluck and enthusiasm. Jonathan thought his youthful, untainted vigor refreshing and sweet.

As usual, the hour was drawing late. Zach left to get his coat at coat check and I soon followed. When I got there, I thought Zach had already left, but instead I found him getting the bum’s rush from inside the coat check area. Initially I assumed he had lost his claim check and went in to help them find his coat, but apparently, the cigarette break the coat room attendant took was too long and Zach in full military zeal, charged into the coat area to leave no jacket behind. I didn’t realize until that moment just how plastered he was, but I guess the four drinks he had before he arrived at the bar were just too much for his system to bear.

I really should have gone with him to make sure he got home okay, but by the time I told Jonathan I was leaving too, Zach was gone into the night. He ended up sending me a text message in the morning which confirmed that he did in fact get home safely. I said good night to Jonathan hastily and dashed out to find a cab to take me to Grand Central. Mike was already waiting on the drunk train to join me on the long journey home.

As I bounced along sixth avenue in the back of the cab trying to ignore the cab TV in the back, it occurred to me that I probably should have made sure Jonathan got home safely too. I really am not a very good friend. Especially since I suspected he was quite intoxicated too. That was only confirmed for me a few minutes later when he sent me a text message of regret that we hadn't dueted to something from *Xanadu*.

But by then, suddenly, the wheels were in motion on the train leaving the station. There will be other nights for two bad singers to duet. *Xanadu* isn't going anywhere, and neither is our friendship. And that's the great thing about a bar like Pieces, and old friends too. You can leave it just where it is and come back, even a few years later and find it exactly the way you left it.

Out With The New

Monday, December 17th - I think watching old movies might be dangerous for me.

The Hollywood writer's strike has been going on for weeks now and it has finally caught up with us on the small screen. We are fresh out of fresh episodes of our favorite shows. And while some shows will be starting or returning in January (*Lost, New Adventures Of Old Christine, American Idol* and a thousand other reality/game shows), the momentum built up so far this fall is at an end. As an avid TV viewer, this has put me in a terrible quandary. What am I supposed to do with all this free time and my incredibly honed staring skills?

It is with this in mind that I have recently returned to watching old movies. What can I say? I am a homo, and I love an old movie. Last month was Guest Programmer month on TCM and even though I have long owned *The Letter* on DVD, I have never actually watched it. But I did TIVO guest programmer Gore Vidal and that film last month and finally this weekend, at a loss for new TV, settled in to watch it. I enjoyed it far more than I thought I would.

I have seen the enormously famous opening and closing scenes a million times, but the whole movie in between was a swift and engaging good time. Somerset Maugham (who I have decided might be my new favorite dead playwright, knowing now that he also wrote the source material for the hilarious *Being Julia* with Annette Bening) wrote the original play and it starts off rather delightfully with a quiet night on a rubber plantation interrupted by Bette Davis plugging six bullets into a man trying desperately to get away from her.

It is all shot very dramatically and powerfully and I thought William Wyler might have used his best tricks in the first two minutes, but the overall film remained sensational right up to Bette's famous final declaration, "With all my heart, I still love the man I killed. Gore said the film still gives him chills, which at his age could honestly be caused by almost anything. But as much as I liked the film, I fear it might stay with me the way other recent old movies have.

I am well known as a soft touch when it comes to the movies. I might have gone to see the most-awful *Deep End of the Ocean* with Michelle Pfeiffer because I cried twice during the trailer ("Children don't get lost. People lose them!"). As much as I love a good comedy, I think I love to cry at a movie even more. I like it best when I cry at a movie you would least expect tears from, like the unexpectedly poignant ending of the Albert Brooks comedy *Defending Your Life*. After all, there is no challenge in crying at something like *Dumbo*, easily the most gut-wrenching 64 minutes ever committed to celluloid, although it is satisfying just the same.

This week on my train ride, I settled back in to watch an old favorite, *National Velvet,* with a young and powerfully earnest Elizabeth Taylor. You can see instantly in the movie why she became a star and her clarity of character is staggering, especially in her scenes with Anne Revere who plays her mother. Taylor breaks your heart in every scene, her pure faith in that wild horse never wavers, and I can usually wring at least five or six cries out of every showing. Even jammed in the drunk train home on Friday night, I freely let the tears flow for all to see. And this is part of the problem.

I let myself become overly involved in these movies, even to points where I don't realize they are influencing me. I am just too susceptible. Years ago in Los Angeles, my roommate Eric and I were shopping for wine at Trader Joe's and I picked out a bottle.

"I've heard good things about this one," I said, not being a wine drinker myself.

"No you haven't." Eric replied flatly, "There is a billboard for it outside our apartment."

The moving images on the screen are even more of a draw to me than a flat advertisement under the warm California sun. Eight weeks after a chance purchase of *Christmas In Connecticut* with Barbara Stanwyck last December and dozens of viewings in a row later, I abandoned my perfectly comfortable Manhattan apartment for a house in the country with a bay window, a fireplace and a piano. I guess compared to buying a whole house, running around all the time saying "I know men. Some of my best friends are men" in a throaty rendition of Tallulah Bankhead in *Lifeboat* isn't so bad, but the end result is the same.

Maybe the problem is that I feel out of control in the whole process, in my whole life really. The movies are long since finished and in the can, but my life is still malleable and open to broad interpretation. I know how a movie will end, but I never know how things will go in my own life. Surprises happen in real life, like they did last night.

Jonathan invited me over to watch the finale of *Survivor*. We are both avid viewers and when he suggested watching the finale together, it certainly seemed like a better idea than spending my Sunday night at home alone. After the *Scene It* party, I knew Mike would never come back to another party at Jonathan's so I came on my own. When I arrived for what I assumed would be another big, loud, gay party, I found Jonathan alone in his living room. I was taken aback.

Slowly over the past few weeks, during classic movie banter by text message and email, a slew of Scrabulous games on Facebook, and a few nights out on the town, I found myself more and more drawn to Jonathan.

It was so different than the situation with D-A-N, or with anyone I had ever experienced before. Yes, D-A-N was classic movie star handsome, but that was all that he was. The thought of pursuing a romantic relationship with him just felt like going through the motions. But Jonathan was different.

Here was someone who was so like me, but at the same time, so much more. Yes, we agreed on movies and TV shows and music and politics and a million subjects, but when I spoke with him, I felt my world expanding. He had his own insights that instantly felt like my own. He did the *New York Times* crossword in ink, something I would never be brave enough to attempt on my own. Jonathan had drive and ambition, and most importantly, he made me laugh. I really felt there was something going on, a deep well of emotion I had never experienced before and I felt myself pulled as if by gravity deeper and deeper into the abyss. In five weeks it felt like I had met my best friend, my soul mate, the love of my life. And I didn't know what to do. This was new. And scary.

Was it even possible that he felt the same about me? He didn't give any real outward signs of being interested in me romantically, but we were as thick as thieves. My own self doubt crept in, those nagging thoughts you have, like walking into a new school for the first time and wondering if you will ever have a friend there. But Jonathan seemed to get me on a level that no one else did, and I really felt like I got him. It was kismet. And when I walked into his apartment last night, it was the first time we had ever really been alone.

We settled in on the couch next to each other for three hours of certain entertainment. As the evening wore on, I drew closer to him. I put my head on his shoulder. I accented my comments with playful touches. Nothing too forward but he would definitely have to be rock dense to not see where things were in my mind. Like all of our times together, it was great.

As I started to leave at the end of the evening, Jonathan approached me cautiously. He let me know very gently that my not subtle signals were received but there would be no reply in kind. As he spoke, the deep well of emotion I felt enveloped me in its blackness. I nodded vigorously and agreed with him, anything to get out of that apartment as soon as possible. He hugged me good bye and I tore out of there like the room was on fire.

I walked the lonely few blocks from his East Village apartment to my car parked just outside the K-Mart. Once locked safely inside, I put my head down on the steering wheel and just cried. It is one of the great things about Manhattan that you can just break down emotionally almost anywhere and strangers will leave you alone. I tried to have enough dignity to make it to the car, but even though I did not look up or around, I know as a New Yorker that people went on about their business all around me as if nothing was happening.

In the long car ride home, all I wanted to do was call someone and tell them what had happened. How I had this wonderful crush on just the best guy in the world and how he rejected my feelings. But as I drove away from the scene of the crime, the only person I wanted to call and tell was Jonathan. He wasn't just some guy I had a crush on. He was my best friend. The person in the world I was the most close to, and at the moment I needed him the most, he was the one person I couldn't call.

I thought about the advice the mother gives in *National Velvet*:

"Win or lose. It's all the same. And how you take it that counts. And knowing when to let go. Knowing when it's over and time to go on to the next thing. Things come suitable to the time. Enjoy each thing and then forget it and go on to the next. There is a time for everything."

So I guess now is the time for me to not be with Jonathan. I will try to tell myself that it is for the best, even if no part of me is willing to believe that. And perhaps I should be using this time to sort out my own emotional state before I start inserting myself into the emotional states of others.

I will watch old movies, and sit in the window box of my room and write while the deer and squirrels roam through the yard like extras in a Douglas Sirk movie. And then at some point, it will be time for me to do something else. When a movie ends, you know it is coming and, especially if you have seen it before, you know what to expect. But life is not like in the movies. It's unexpected and it isn't over until it's over.

Phoenix Rising

Saturday, December 22nd – I have spent the past week trying to not think about Jonathan. I made a decision to concentrate on myself and my quiet life in suburbia. Well, yesterday a deer wandered right up to the bay window in the front of the house and was giving a disapproving glance at my Christmas tree when I spotted her from the kitchen. I really felt for a moment like I was in the Douglas Sirk movie of my dreams, and not just because light was coming in from every direction at once. But when I went to get my camera, Mike scared the poor animal away.

This is what passes for excitement and high drama at my house, and it does provide fleeting moments of distraction from my thoughts. But I am only human so you will understand why I took a trip to a grungy watering hole in the East Village on a Friday night instead of linger in a bay window waiting for all of God's creatures to stroll by in Technicolor. Besides, grungy bar or not, I couldn't resist the urge to see Jonathan one last time before he flew home for the holidays and out of my life for the time being.

I wonder if grungy is really the right word for the Phoenix, an alt-boy neighborhood bar in the East Village. Seedy doesn't seem appropriate because I never worry about losing my wallet. And it isn't disgusting like The Cock, which in its past location had a bathroom so filthy I preferred instead to urinate outside against a wrought iron fence. That dump really knew how to put the anus in tetanus.

Since then, the Cock moved with no small irony into the bowels of another dirty old building in the former location of a bar called the Hole (that, as they say, fits), but I haven't been there since it moved. I'll just wait for the Health Inspector's final report and a booster shot.

The director Richard Brooks told a great story about making *The Blackboard Jungle* at MGM and how he wanted it to be "gritty" so, for instance, he had them make the walls near the light switches dirty, like in a real life high school. But every night, the old craftsmen of MGM would dutifully paint everything back to a pristine white because that was the MGM way. Most Manhattan gay bars are sophisticated and pristine, like an old MGM movie, as are the fussy young queens who go to them.

But the Phoenix is gritty, yes that's the word I want, but in just the same manufactured way the *Pirates of the Caribbean* ride at Disneyland is dangerous. There is graffiti on the bathroom walls, but it's all very clever and occasionally political or deeply thought. There is a gruff bear of a man in the basement, but he is polite and runs the coat check. So the gay boys can have their sense of life in an old fashioned road house, but still order a fancy mixed drink without getting punched in the face.

The Christmas holiday is right around the corner and that means everyone is escaping the island of Manhattan like it's Paris 1940 and the Nazis are about to march in. And in much the same way, the gays like to have one last drink before they fly off to fly over places where mind-numbing conversations will take place in living rooms crowded with knick knacks and oppressive memories, and the last gay person they will see for a week will be a weary flight attendant more interested in his own frosted tips than your safety in the air.

Mike had just said good bye to his mother, who visited us for a week instead of the other way around, and he was certainly in the mood for a night of East Village boys, his favorite kind. I invited him along even though I had really invited myself along. Terry and Jonathan had hatched a plan to hang out there together, but since they hatched the plan on my own Facebook Wall, I felt no compunction about inviting myself and a few friends along as well.

As it turns out, that was the right move, as a little rain earlier had caused Cinderella to meet her midnight a little earlier than planned and Terry bailed on the whole thing. That would have left Jonathan alone to hunt his neighborhood haunt, and we can't let that happen, can we? Not right before Christmas! And not while I am harboring this not-at-all secret crush on him that I am trying to force myself to accept is just a friend thing.

I invited Zach to come along who insisted he would stay away from the gin and tonic this time around. He brought along his very newly single friend Jon, who looked very familiar to us all, but mostly looked like Zach in five years. The conversation spun easily between the five of us into a roundelay, layering over and over again in its series of recurring themes (the pending election, gay life, *30 Rock*, Britney, Manhattan), while past acquaintances of Jonathan's made blatant overtures for rematches that he oh so coyly moved to the txt realm or rebuffed entirely. How polite of him to do that for my sake, I thought, even as I saw no gain for myself there. Meanwhile, Mike was struck by Zach's powerful and rigid stoicism, more than a match for his own blank visage. Jon was bored, and I passed the time waiting to see who I would run into at the bar.

I don't know many people in New York City, and I infrequently go to the Phoenix. But it never fails that someone I know is in that bar! This time around it was Michael, Melissa's contortionist of a roommate, who had shaved his head and packed on easily thirty pounds of muscle. If I were living back in Los Angeles, I would assume that he got a part in a movie and had altered himself for a character role, but in New York, even though he might well be an actor preparing for his Broadway debut, it seemed more likely that he just was tired of the old Michael and decided to make a drastic change. Having worn the same hair style for twenty years now, it is a notion I don't easily understand.

In the end, it turns out that everything else with me was still exactly the same. Outside the coat check, a now drunken Jonathan confronted me about my electric blue polo shirt. “I know why you wear blue all the time,” he smiled as though revealing a surprising secret. But it was no secret to either of the blue-eyed people in the conversation, whose own vanity led them to the matching color.

We got into a competition about the blueness of each other's eyes and I insisted on one-upping him by telling him that my eyes change color with the color around them. Then with great effect, I zipped up my pale grey jacket and Jonathan watched my blue eyes turn pale grey. “I hate you,” he said as he turned on his heel and stumbled up the stairs.

It is true that I am often an enormously unlikeable person. I don't know why anyone listens to our radio show. I tell Romaine all the time that we are two of the most unlikeable people ever and then we just laugh about how silly it all is. Maybe people like us together because we are both so horrible that we deserve each other.

Out in the real world, my terrible personality keeps my number of close friends conveniently small and my desire to leave the house even smaller. I want to be with Jonathan, but clearly my yearning desires are no match for my hostility and unrelenting sense of competition, certain death in gay romantic circles. But this is who I am, and gritty as it may be, it has gotten me pretty far in life, just not this night, in this bar, with this man.

But as long as I have a blog to write and a radio show to do, I will continue to burn my way through modern gay life, rise from the ashes once more, and do it all again the next week. Jonathan is gone for now but he will be back in the New Year and I will either be over him or take a second bite at the apple.

After all, it is winter, and we have to keep warm somehow.

Jingle Balls II: Escape Clause

Friday, December 28th - You may recall my frank discussion of my balls some weeks back. Well, I have some resolution to the story. Just in time for the holidays! Because nothing says holiday cheer like discussing your scrotum in public.

The final step in the process was a review of the situation by the urologist. I have never been to the urologist in my life. Why should I? The junk works, so why mess with perfection? As usual, in need of a doctor, I rummaged around on the internet for a while and then picked someone with a catchy name who was nearby. I suppose I could check credentials or something, but I have to assume a total quack would not be able to afford to pay rent in one of the most expensive cities in the world if he didn't know what he was doing. And yes, I did specifically choose a male urologist. It is weird enough having a stranger manhandle me under fluorescent lighting, I don't need to make it completely bizarre by bringing a woman into the mix.

The doctor I chose was in Gramercy Park, steps away from my regular doctor and a convenient subway stop. He is right around the corner from the National Arts Club, which when I passed it reminded me that it had been a long time since I saw *Manhattan*

Murder Mystery, so I picked it up on DVD. I had to wait seven weeks for my appointment, and even though my doctor told me it was probably nothing and the two women at the ultrasound office couldn't even find what I was talking about, I was still filled with a certain level of anxiety.

I had my appointment in the week before Christmas. I trotted down to his office and sat in the waiting room filled with current magazines and old men for about 45 minutes before he finally saw me. The urologist looks like all doctors in Woody Allen movies: tall, reed thin and expressionless. He also spoke with a German accent, but not like a character actor in a Hollywood movie about Nazis. He sounded more like a mad professor in an old Looney Tunes cartoon (although visually lacking the mess of white hair and the cheesy Frito Bandito moustache). The whole package instantly filled me with confidence, as all situations that remind me of the movies do.

He asked me the usual routine questions, even though I had written them all out on the form in the waiting room.

"How many zexual partners: zingle or multiple?"

"Um. Right now, or over my lifetime?"

"In your lifetime."

"Oh. Multiple."

He arched his eyebrow and gave me an ever so disapproving murmur. I was instantly outraged and defensive about what a slut I have been. You know what. I am a sexually active 38 year old man. I don't need to get shit from some stranger about the fact that I have had sex with more than one person in my whole life. Granted, the number isn't two. But how does he know that? If I want to feel judged, I'll go to a department store cosmetics counter and put my head inside the black light box with the magnifying mirror in it that makes you buy anything they put in front of you. I don't need to hear it from the man who is going to tell me definitively if I have cancer.

So he sends me off to the waiting room while his assistant contacts my doctor to have my records faxed over. After that he calls me down to the separate exam room.

"Take your pants down and I will take a look."

I kick off my shoes and then start in on my pants when he stops me.

"You can leave your shoes on. I von't be examining your feet."

So, like James Edstrom in the Ramble, I just shoved my pants down around my ankles and hopped (quite literally) onto the table. I laid back as instructed and he began to dispassionately knead my balls like bread dough.

"Zo. What do you do for a living?"

Really? A conversation about the wonders of satellite radio while you are all over my balls like a case of the crabs? This is definitely one of those situations, like when standing at a urinal, where I am not in the mood for idle chit chat. He asked me where the lump was that I felt, and when I told him, he stopped the exam as suddenly as he began.

"What is behind and above the left testicle is a normal structure. Put your pants back on please and see me in my office," he declared as he ripped his surgical gloves off dramatically and dispensed with them in the trash can nearby. He just left me lying on the table with my pants down around my ankles. I felt so vulnerable!

Once I pulled myself and my outfit (such as it was) together, I went back to his office. He glanced over my paperwork and looked up at me. "There is nothing going on in your genitals." He stated it so flatly I instantly wanted a second opinion. It was the second meanest thing a doctor has told me during this ordeal, only behind my regular doctor assuring me that I have nothing to worry about because "testicular cancer is a disease of young men." I don't need a stranger to tell me there is nothing going on in my genitals. I live with them. I know what they are doing at night.

Unfortunately, my ultrasound results weren't there, so he insisted that I come back on Monday for a follow-up. Monday, as in Christmas Eve. Aren't Jewish doctors the best? I guess he doesn't like movies and Chinese food. However, it did take seven weeks for the initial appointment and he is on the American Board of Urology, so I guess I should take whatever appointment I can get. I trotted back down to the city on Christmas Eve, waited once again in his waiting room with several of the same loose characters I saw during my initial visit. He called me in, glanced over my ultrasound, and then waved his hand over it as if performing a magic spell.

"Nothing. There is nothing here. Go home. Enjoy your time. Have fun. I will see you in six months. Maybe there will be something there then."

And with that my testicular cancer ordeal was over. As definitive as the Supreme Court ruling in Bush Vs. Gore, the process was stopped dead in its tracks. Yes, maybe something else will go wrong in my genitals, but as I will be six months older during the next go round, I am that much further away from testicular cancer. So now there is nothing left to do but sit back, enjoy Diane Keaton reunited with Woody Allen and pronounce my personal Manhattan mystery solved.

All About Eve

Tuesday, January 1st – "Is this the most over-hyped night of the year or what?" Cyd Zeigler asked rhetorically at Henry's swank New Year's Eve party. For me, it is often the most dreaded night of the year. So much sweating and anticipation. Where to go. Who to go with. Forced to drink champagne against your will and then stumble through the virtually incomprehensible auld Scottish lyrics of Auld Lang Syne. And for what? To see how Dick Clark is fairing since his stroke? Note that Anderson Cooper and Ryan Seacrest seem to revel in working the holiday since they can assiduously avoid kissing anyone personal at midnight? It's all just a lot of show. No wonder the older I get, the more I just want to stay home in bed.

On Friday night, Mike and I met up with Cyd and his wonderful boyfriend Dan at Barracuda. Earlier in the evening, I had been roped into hours of joyous heterosexual mayhem by Elaine Miles, the best friend of my half sister Laura. I had sipped $600-a-bottle red wine while I came to realize from their foreign party rituals that I don't spend much time in groups of straight people anymore. It was a bit like discovering a lost civilization. But moments later, a cab had whisked me down to homo town and I was back in my noisy, ass-grabby element.

Cyd and Dan are a sensational couple with a romantic love story straight out of 1940s MGM. Like *Enchanted Cottage* with homosexuality but without the disfigurement. Unfortunately, our work schedules are so dramatically different it is rare that we get to spend much time together. So when they suggested Mike and I join them at a party on New Year's Eve, we jumped at the chance. As it was, we had headed out on Friday night to pick up copies of the local gay bar rag HX for some ideas of what to do on the big night.

Going to a house party with Cyd and Dan was the perfect solution. A room full of strangers but also a couple of built-in reliable conversationalists too. Even Mike, who hates meeting new people and going to parties, seemed to approve of the idea. And, we figured, if the party sucked, we could always wander down to Therapy and have a few drinks in public. As if to make our plans even more fateful, on New Year Eve, the drunk trains run well past their usual killjoy time of 1:50am, guaranteeing us an easy way home no matter when we wanted to call it all quits.

In between our encounters with Cyd and Dan, we enjoyed a quiet weekend at home, exactly the kind of existence I had hoped for when I first saw the house almost one year ago. But then late on Sunday night the spell over my own enchanted cottage was broken when Mike came up from putting his laundry in the washer and reported that there was some water running from the haunted bathroom in the basement, across the concrete floor and down into the center drain there. I knew immediately that it could only mean one thing: the sewer line was clogged. The haunted bathroom sits over the access point to the sewer line, so if there is a problem, the toilet overflowing there is the canary in the coal mine. Not putting two and two together, Mike left the washer running and, as it drained, the trickle of water from the bathroom turned into a sweet torrent of water, toilet paper and shit.

Trying to find a plumber on the Sunday night of a holiday weekend was going to be difficult and expensive. An hour or so later a very nice man arrived and charged me a very pretty penny. He spent five minutes snaking out roots from the massive tree in my front yard, handed me a receipt and left. My house was designed to withstand a nuclear winter, but by planting a tree over the sewer line and under the power line, the builder guaranteed a lifetime of expensive homeowner headaches. Sometimes, even the best of planning can lead to unintended self-sabotage.

We spent the rest of our Sunday evening cleaning up the mess, which was disgusting to say the least. It seemed like an apt way to end an imperfect year. Purchasing the house had taken all sorts of unforeseen tolls on me, and this was just the final indignation. The irony wasn't lost on me that after one of our primary motivations for leaving the Harlem apartment was having more bathrooms that it would be a bathroom itself that would suddenly muck up my life. I loved living there but everything has a price. Suffice it to say, when I emerged from my bedroom the next morning, I was done wringing out mops and was ready to ring out the year instead.

So that afternoon Mike and I headed off into the city with a bottle of champagne and a bottle of vodka in a brown paper bag. Mike thought we should have put it in more discreet packaging, but since it was December 31st, I think everyone knew exactly what we were carrying. Plus Mike brought along mini bottles of rum to warm us up along the way. He chugged his as a shot before boarding the train, but I kept mine in my pocket. By the time we got to the city, my short nap on the Metro North Train made me hungry. Unfortunately, everything in Harlem was closed except for our tried and true Popeye's Chicken. I ordered a chicken strip combo, and poured my mini bottle of rum into my medium Coke and drank it on our way down to the party near Columbia University.

We got to the party and it was in a very glamorous new building with fresh wood paneling in the elevator that Mike insisted on sniffing like he was a junkie and the elevator car was made of modeling glue. We hung up our coats and wandered into the sea of cute guys. We struck gold! It was just the right party to be at: tons of food and booze and cuteness. We set about immediately to get smashed off our asses.

It turns out that Henry, our party host, wasn't a stranger since I met (and lusted after him) at a karaoke night with Cyd some months earlier. Mike knew instantly that I liked him because he was completely my type, although he wasn't the only one. There was a cute guy named Justin acting as one of the party hosts and he was also adorably blondie-pie, though in a different way from Henry. Henry looks more like Daniel Craig as James Bond minus 20 years of rough living, while Justin looks like Torrance's unsupportive college boyfriend in *Bring It On*. Justin was very solicitous to everyone in the room, so it was impossible to feel special when he would get kissy and grabby. It was still welcome though. Turns out he was 28, not 22 as I first unhappily suspected, and for most of the evening I believed that he had an equally adorable boyfriend hosting with him named Dan, who didn't seem to mind how flirty he was with everyone. But he probably didn't mind because Dan was Henry's boyfriend, not Justin's.

The party was in full swing for hours after the ball dropped, but Cyd and Dan were ready to drop before 1am. Once they left, Mike and I kept drinking and tried to meet a few of the other drunken strangers at the party. I got into a deep discussion about developing nations and how clean water programs, the Life Straw (perhaps *the* innovation of the early 21st century) and Heifer International lay the groundwork for economic development with a guy who specialized in such things but probably preferred to make out than explain the complexities of emerging economies in Africa to a drunk college dropout. I was just trying to show an interest in his work, which did not interest him in me at all. Later, we ran into a friend of Cyd's named Sergio, who had initially been driven away by our feverish discussion of the pending Iowa caucus. We do like our deep discussions at shallow gay parties, don't we?

Much drunker and later, Sergio took a second crack at us and found a much lighter conversation going on. The discussion evaporated entirely when we decided to make out instead of chat. And let me tell you, it was just what the doctor ordered. I didn't get his number. I didn't want to go home with him. I just wanted to spend a few moments at a party talking about nothing (his favorite color is red) and kissing intermittently. After all, it is New Year's Eve. The night of the year designed for making out with a stranger. And so much better than the year I randomly made out with Paul's friend Manfred after he had thrown up in the gutter outside Revolver. However, all good things must come to an end. Mike and I left to take one of the drunk trains home and I gave Sergio one last good kiss good bye. And that was the end of that.

Now boozed up but good and happy after an hour of canoodling, I sailed into Grand Central Station and fell in love once again with its simple grandeur and the thrill of the crowd. No one told me but it turns out that Grand Central is *the* place to be on New Year's Eve after midnight. In lieu of striking clocks and abandoned glass slippers, it is a sea of hot young drunk straight guys, smiling and having a blast. Everyone is infused with the joy of the night, boisterous and friendly, waiting for their respective trains home.

The party continued on our train, although it quieted somewhat as one by one, the passengers passed out in their seats. We did get caught at one station while the police were called aboard to deal with some belligerent passengers. Later, an attractive red-headed woman ran into her old friends who were sitting around us. The boys had given her the charming moniker "butt lice" and it was "butt lice" herself who explained that her friends had been the rowdy boys who had been pulled off the train. Another local mystery solved, although the origin of her nickname remains purposefully unknown.

A little after six AM, the train pulled into the station and as expected, there were no taxis waiting when we arrived. So, Mike and I made our drunken way on foot up the hill that leads to the house. Dawn was just starting to break and the town was covered in a slight foggy haze, blurred considerably at the edges by my drunkenness. By the time we walked up the crest of the hill and turned into the driveway, the dawn's early light was making its way slowly through the clouds, dramatically lighting the night sky above the bare tree branches and filling the yard with an eerie blue glow. It was all so beautiful to come home to. My home.

Eight is my lucky number, I thought optimistically, as I tumbled into bed. And this year is 2008. So maybe this will be the year it will all fall together. This will be the year my luck returns in force, and all the pieces fit together the way they should. I already got a little lucky at the party, so there is no reason to think that kind of luck won't last all year long.

I pulled the covers up to my head, nestled into my sea of pillows and drifted off to sleep with visions of my happy new year to come. An imperfect year, certainly, but just the perfect ending to a perfect New Year's Eve.

Acknowledgements

Perhaps privacy and discretion are out-dated in our new cyber universe, as web profiles and social networks now broadcast our every movement. To me, no site was ever better at helping turn a random meeting in a bar into a treasure trove of stalker-worthy info than Friendster. This book would have been impossible without Friendster's easy search function and the natural inclination for people to provide too much information about themselves online.

Still, when people head out on the town for an evening of fun, most of them have some expectation of privacy. That is, of course, if they don't run into me.

I have a habit of writing about my family, friends, and even total strangers, online and more recently in print, and making it all available for the entire world to see. Most of the people in my life are private citizens, if not private people. But over the years, they have graciously allowed me to put a certain amount of their business out in public as I tell the story of my own life. For this, I must humbly thank and acknowledge them all.

More specifically, I have to thank my most private friend (and frequent roommate) Mike. His near constant presence, especially in the last decade since we both moved to New York, has left him regularly mentioned in my writing and even more frequently on my radio show. He insists that I mischaracterize him all the time, so take my impression of him with a grain of salt. Just know: without him, I would never have published a book, let alone washed a dish. So I thank him for both his patience and for his preventing me from slipping into my natural state of being: Later Howard Hughes meets Grey Gardens.

Before working on this book, I hadn't realized how much time I spent with Chi Chi LaRue in 2007. Reliving our adventures together all across the country was a joy. I love Chi Chi's boundless enthusiasm for life and more importantly encouragement for me to write down everything that happened (even if I did politely leave one or two things out).

My family is in every regard the foundation from which the rest of my life grows. I only wish I was around them more, though I cherish the time we do spend together. They have given me the freedom to be myself, and in public no less, and for that I am eternally grateful.

Romaine Patterson has grown over the years from a co-worker to one of my closest confidants. We are as thick as thieves and heaven help the person who gets between us. As much as it is our job to talk about ourselves and our lives, I appreciate her respecting my boundaries when I ask her to, and forgiving me when I cross all of hers.

Much of this book coincided with meeting many new people in 2007. Knowing me such a short time and still putting up with me, I must thank those people especially. If I wrote about you, it is because I think you are hot or interesting or both. And if I failed to mention you, I'm sorry. I was probably drunk and just forget. In either case, please don't take it all too personally.

It goes without saying that Ben Harvey is a wonderful and devoted friend for whom I would journey to the ends of the earth if asked, although I am grateful he has never needed me to go further than Brooklyn.

Finally, I have the uncanny ability to relive strong emotions (even years later) with such intensity that people often think they just happened. This has never been truer for me than it is with the person who closes this book: Jonathan. With him, The End was only the beginning of a more complex tale that does not wind up with happily ever after.

Finishing up this book felt like an eternity for me. I just didn't want to have to revisit all those emotions again from our first few weeks of knowing each other. But to not include him would be impossible. He was then, and continues to be, an essential part of the story of my life. This book would not be complete without him.

Jonathan is an extraordinary person. He is my favorite person. And I have no regrets, only love. He is all I need, but I need all of him. That we aren't together… I'm shattered. A million pieces from a thousand puzzles caught in the wind. But life happens as it happens. Just as the people around me have no control over what I write about them, so too I have no control over how my story ends.

All I can do is keep going. And so I do.

About The Author

Derek Hartley hosts the GLAAD Award-winning Derek And Romaine with Romaine Patterson on Sirius XM Radio. For eight and a half years, he was a columnist for PlanetOut.com, which inspired his first book *Colonnade: A Life in Columns* (Spacuna Publishing, Oct. 2009). He lives in New York.

Photo by Jeff Eason, Derek Hartley (center) with cover models Erik Rhodes and Christopher Schram.